# Questions of Faith

# Questions of Faith

## Encountering Christ at the Point of Doubt and Confusion

Thomas A. Robinson

Mazarin Press
Raleigh, North Carolina USA

© Copyright 2018 by Thomas A. Robinson

All rights reserved. No part of this publication may be reproduced in any form or by any electronic or mechanical means, including information storage and retrieval systems, without the prior written permission of the author.

Published by:
Mazarin Press
8801 Fast Park Drive, Ste. 301
Raleigh, NC 27617

ISBN: 978-1-7324077-0-1 (print)
ISBN: 978-1-7324077-1-8 (epub)
ISBN: 978-1-7324077-2-5 (mobi)

Printed in the United States

Unless otherwise stated, Scripture quotations are taken from THE HOLY BIBLE, New Revised Standard Version, © Copyright 1989, Division of Christian Education of the National Council of the Churches of Christ in the United States of America. Used by permission.

"The Issue of Abortion: How Things *Really* Are," found on pp. 107, et seq. (Copyright 1995, Thomas A. Robinson) was originally published in *Encounter: Creative Theological Scholarship*, Autumn 1995, vol. 56, no. 4, pp. 335-341).

"The Sunday Buffet" (Copyright 2002, Thomas A. Robinson), and "The Good Friday Tree" (Copyright 1999, Thomas A. Robinson), found on p. 53 and 126, respectively, were originally published in *Dispatches to the Front*, a newsletter of the Riverside Gathering — a post-denominational congregation without walls, centered in Durham, NC.

To Jane, who filled my heart to overflowing when, at high noon on Saturday, August 28, 1971, in response to a liminal "Question of Faith," offered to her by the Rev. Dr. Charles Shannon, looked at me and said, "I will."

# Acknowledgements

As Moses reminds us, we all drink from wells that we did not dig (Deut 6:11, KJV). Gratefully, therefore, I want to acknowledge the debt I owe, not only to Jane and our children — Anna, Walker, Blair & Gray — but to a host of others who have helped me develop this book — often without knowing that you were doing so.

I have been richly blessed by three towering mentors — far more than my equitable share. All now enjoy the fellowship of God's Heavenly Banquet: the late Rev. Dr. Richard Crowder, the late Rev. Fred Falls, and the late Rev. Dr. Wilson Nesbitt. All members of the Western North Carolina Annual Conference (United Methodist Church), they surrounded me with unmerited love, encouragement, and unflinching support over many, many years.

Two friends also quickly come to mind — Luke Bell and Jim Sutherland. For more than 30 years now, each has served as a theological sparring partner, pushing back at me and my often wandering ruminations. In completely different ways, each has spoken truth to me when my mind's eye might otherwise have been deflected.

Through the years, four other close friends have specially graced my life as fellow sojourners: Robert Alexander, Felix Markham,

## Acknowledgements

Ralph Gunderson, and Jim Petrea. For more than 55 years, I have known and been inspired by Robert's deep and abiding faith. Within separate Durham churches, Felix and Ralph have shown so many of us just how important – and powerful – calm devotion can be. Jim has patiently taught me that missional activity *always* requires the crossing of barriers. Indeed, "If we're comfortable, it isn't missional."

Luke Bell and I have reminded ourselves on numerous occasions that we are beneficiaries of the finest theological education available anywhere (Duke Divinity School). Within that special space, a host of serious, devout scholars taught us that one must think not only with the head, but with the heart. Prominent among my Divinity School professors were Tom Langford, Moody Smith, and Bishop Ken Goodson, all now deceased. Equally important to my theological growth and development were/are professors Mickey Efird, Harmon Smith, and Rick Lischer.

I have also been blessed by my association with a number of wonderfully disparate local congregations: Olney Presbyterian (Gastonia, NC), Home Moravian Church (Winston-Salem, NC), Centenary UMC (Winston-Salem, NC), First UMC (Gastonia, NC), Trinity UMC (Durham, NC), Saxapahaw UMC (Saxapahaw, NC), the Riverside Gathering (a post-denominational congregation without walls, centered in Durham, NC), Asbury UMC (Durham, NC), Duke University Chapel, and Trinity Avenue Presbyterian (Durham, NC). Although not always in harmony, each has taught me that the best theology is performed at the congregational level.

Penultimately, I'd like also to acknowledge the debt I owe to a humble, "mere Christian" — my Grandmother Lib — who would scold me if I did not offer my ultimate and final acknowledgment of gratitude to "the LORD, who brought [me] out of Egypt, out of the house of slavery" (Deut 6:12). Indeed, "Thank you, LORD!"

# Foreword

Within these pages, I have sought to engage you within one of my core beliefs — that Christ seeks us out long before we ever seek Him. He meets us at the point of our questions and doubts; He does not wait for us to resolve them. He engages us not only within our hopes and dreams, but within our frustrations.

It is no accident, therefore, that if we look at Holy Scripture, we see this same pattern: that many of our most important lessons come to us upon the tail of a special question — a question of faith. And if we listen closely to those around us, we discover that our faith is also formed and strengthened through questions of faith that are offered by those who travel with us along the Way. Indeed, questions of faith are marvelous. While they almost always elicit answers, those answers often are ones that we don't expect.

Here follows a collection of reflections that flow from questions of faith. Pulled from an informal journal that I've maintained since moving to Durham with Jane and the kids in 1986, they vary in length and style. Three-quarters spring from questions found in Holy Scripture, one-fourth from the tongues of loved ones. It is my sincere belief that if you examine your own journey of faith, you

# Foreword

will see that questions have been an important part of your own framework of faith.

Most of us are an admixture of faith and doubt, a blend of absolute assurance and utter confusion. We sometimes feel a bit like the father of the boy who was filled with the evil spirit [*see* Mark 9:17 *et seq.*]. Jesus says to the man — and to us — "All things can be done for the one who believes." Like the father, we cry out, "I believe; help my unbelief!" (Mark 9:24). The One who gave up His life for us is always happy to oblige! Thanks be to God!

Thomas A. Robinson
Durham, North Carolina
May 25, 2018

# Contents

| | |
|---|---|
| Acknowledgements | vii |
| Foreword | ix |

| | | |
|---|---|---|
| 1. | **Questions** Anyone, Anyone? | 1 |
| 2. | Name-Calling | 7 |
| 3. | **Goin'** to the Holy Land | 15 |
| 4. | **Sioux** City Christmas | 25 |
| 5. | Begrudging Generosity | 33 |
| 6. | A Few Harsh Words | 35 |
| 7. | Love is a Verb! | 41 |
| 8. | It's All in the Voice | 45 |
| 9. | The **Bread Line** | 49 |
| 10. | **The Sunday Buffet** | 53 |
| 11. | **It's** Lunch Time! | 55 |
| 12. | A Favorable Time | 59 |
| 13. | Mary, Mary — Not Contrary | 67 |
| 14. | The Fish that Got Sick to its Stomach | 73 |
| 15. | Centering Prayer | 79 |
| 16. | Seeing as God Sees | 83 |
| 17. | Sojourners | 89 |

## Contents

| | | |
|---|---|---|
| 18. | Death's Defeat! | 97 |
| 19. | Knitting Lessons | 103 |
| 20. | The Issue of Abortion — How Things "Really Are" | 107 |
| 21. | Dead Man Talking: Maundy Thursday and the 11th Commandment | 121 |
| 22. | The Good Friday Tree | 125 |
| 23. | The Power of Love | 129 |
| 24. | Ebb Tide | 131 |
| 25. | Cheers from the Sidelines | 135 |
| 26. | Little Big Man: Zacchaeus' Child-Like Exuberance | 141 |
| 27. | Prom Night | 145 |
| 28. | The Lion and the Hen | 151 |
| 29. | Mary, Darlin', How Does Your Garden Grow? | 155 |
| 30. | Simeon's Story | 159 |
| 31. | The Prophet Peggy | 163 |
| 32. | **Waiting for the Lord** | **169** |

About the Author     173

# 1

# Questions Anyone, Anyone?

*"Lord, if another member of the church sins against me, how often should I forgive? As many as seven times?"*

Questions form an integral part of our everyday lives. Questions may be as solicitous as a greeting — "How are you?" They can be as combative as an accusation — "Didn't you do that on purpose?" Questions may actually be more important than their corresponding answers, for a poorly worded question leads generally to an ambiguous answer.

Sometimes our questions are so full of information that they provide as much insight about us, the questioner, as they do about the person who is to respond. Often, we think we know the answer to our question before we even verbalize it. We ask the question not so much as to gain an answer, but instead, to bring home a point. We all remember that little boy or little girl in third grade who always had a hand in the air and when he or she was recognized, the question was spoken by the child not so much to get an answer — the child already knew it — but rather to make the child look smart in front of the rest of us.

Sometimes the answer to our question can take us by surprise. We see such a surprising response from our Lord as he encountered Peter one day.

> Then Peter came and said to him, "Lord, if another member of the church sins against me, how often should I forgive? As many as seven times?" Jesus said to him, "Not seven times, but, I tell you, seventy-seven times" (Matt. 18:21-22).

In a way, Peter was like our third-grade questioner. He thought he had a good idea as to what the response to his question would be. No doubt Peter would have remembered that according to the Jewish law of that time, one was required to forgive another once, twice, or even thrice — but not four times. Peter had clearly come part of the way in understanding the nature of the Kingdom of God, as declared by Jesus Christ, and its rigorous demands of discipleship, for in suggesting that we ought to forgive seven times, Peter had more than doubled the old standard.

Peter may have expected to be praised by Jesus for the liberality of his viewpoint, but instead of receiving the anticipated praise, Peter is surprised by the answer of his Lord. We are to forgive seventy-seven times, says Jesus — meaning that we are not to keep score at all. We are to forgive and forgive and forgive, and when we have been wronged again by our offender, we are still to forgive, without consideration of how many times we have suffered to forgive.

Perhaps it could be argued that such an attitude of forgiveness by Jesus makes a mockery of any standards that have been set for behavior. After all, if we are continuously to forgive the offense of another, have we not in fact abrogated the standard we seek to hold up as proper conduct and behavior? Indeed, if we are to continue to forgive, has not the standard been totally lost?

Viewed against the backdrop of the Matthew text, the response of Jesus to Peter is consistent and clear. Jesus' requirement that we continuously and unceasingly forgive is our only fitting response to the action of God in forgiving us of our sins against God and our fellow men and women. It is the only proper reaction to a brother or sister who has wronged us.

We should not be so surprised by the answer of Jesus to Peter because Jesus has already given an unconventional demand to us when we have been wronged. How many of us, when we have been truly wronged by our neighbor, retreat to our private sanctuary and lick our wounds? And how many of us enjoy donning the cape of the martyr when we have been poorly treated by those around us? Isn't there something about our nature that delights in the attention we receive when we have been hurt by the actions of another?

We do not have to recall the Bactine® commercials from decades ago to realize that as children we enjoyed our mother's attention to our skinned knee. As we grow older, we do not run to mother when we have been wronged, but we do often languish in our pain or sorrow nevertheless. Jesus' first requirement when we have been wronged is a difficult one. We are to cast aside our hurt feelings and approach the person who has wronged us (Matt. 18:15). Jesus places the burden of initiating reconciliation *not on the one who has done the wrong*, as we might argue and expect it to be, but on the one who has suffered.

To this "burden" Jesus adds the requirement of privacy. We are not to tell the world how we have been wronged. We are not to spread news of the evil act to those around us but are instead to seek reconciliation *quietly* with the person who has done us damage. Even if we are rejected by the wrongdoer, we are not free to gossip about the other's conduct. We are to take one or two others with us to attempt again to gain a healed and reconciled relationship

(*See* Matt. 18:16). If our brother or sister still does not become reconciled to us we are to bring it before the church (Matt. 18:17). Even here there is an element of privacy, for Jesus does not say that we are to broadcast the situation, but rather we are to hope that the actions of the community of believers may bring about the healing.

At each point in this process the need for healing is central, not our need for sympathy and comfort. When an action causes one of our group harm, it has caused harm to the entire community and the goal of each step in the process detailed by Jesus is the regaining of the equilibrium that existed before the wrong was committed.

Why are we to expend such extraordinary energy to effect reconciliation? Why does Jesus require us to forgive without counting the number of times we have already forgiven? In the face of the action of God in forgiving all our sins, healing our diseases, redeeming our lives from utter despair and from the burdens of our active transgressions against God and our neighbor, how can we respond otherwise? How can we continue to dote on ourselves and refuse to make every effort to communicate forgiveness to those around us when God has already taken our sin and removed it from us as far as East is from West?

The answer to this question is, of course, very simple; we can't. The answer of Jesus to Peter does not make a mockery of our standards. To the contrary, this sort of action, on the part of the wounded, takes quite seriously not only the violation, but the violator.

Peter's forgiveness question comes at the close of a parable known as the Parable of the Good Shepherd. That parable is important, particularly since, within the pages of this book, we are talking about questions. In those verses Jesus asks an important hypothetical question: "If a shepherd has a hundred sheep, and one of them has gone astray, does he not leave the ninety-nine on the mountains and go in search for the one that went astray?" (Matt. 18:12).

We've heard the question so many times that we answer without thinking and in doing so we probably answer the question incorrectly. Let me repeat Jesus' question, "If a shepherd has a hundred sheep, and one of them has gone astray, does he not leave the ninety-nine on the mountains and go in search for the one that went astray?"

Our honest answer is that, of course, *he doesn't*. It's probably the same sheep that wandered off last week and if we go find him or her, the sheep will probably only wander off again next week. If you owned a flock of sheep, would you trust that flock to a shepherd who'd risk the ninety-nine to try to find one? It isn't good business. If the shepherd stopped to read the shepherding office manual, it would tell him never to take such a stupid risk. Today's retail stores would be marvelously happy if they could limit inventory shrinkage to one percent.

The point of Jesus' question is that the love of God is exactly *unlike* the love of the shepherd. When all would give up on us, God does not. And if God is so intent upon finding the one sheep who has strayed from communion with the others, we are to do likewise. If God is so busy forgiving us our trespasses, the least we can do is forgive those who trespass against us. And so, we are to seek out those who seem lost, for without the Grace of God, we *all are lost*. And when we find that lost sheep, we are to forgive without worrying whether it is the fifth or even the one thousandth time we have had to take him or her back.

# 2

# Name-Calling

"And ought not this woman, a daughter of Abraham whom Satan bound for eighteen years, be loosed from this bond on the Sabbath day?"

On the morning of April 17, 1949, a young woman in Gaston County, North Carolina, gave birth to a son. Neither the woman nor her husband had the benefit of class, privilege, or education. Barely literate, they were second-generation textile workers, making a few dollars each week while breathing cotton dust, tied to a mill village in much the same way that medieval serfs had been tied to the manor.

Her life-giving labors accomplished, the woman talked with her husband about the name that would be given to their son. He'd been born on Easter Sunday. They determined to choose something that would commemorate the magical moment of birth and regeneration on such a special day. And so, they named their newborn son..., "Bunny." True story: they named him Bunny.

I first saw Bunny on the playground during the first week of my first grade in elementary school. Bunny was two years older than my twin brother and me. On that particular morning, we heard there was a good fight out back on the playground and so we ran around the corner of the building to see Bunny beating up a fifth grader who'd made fun of his name. As you can imagine, by the time Bunny was in the third grade, he'd had many opportunities to "discuss" the moniker given to him by his parents.

Names — they can be powerful; they can be burdensome. They can be cruel. Perhaps you grew up knowing a "Fatso." Or worse, perhaps you grew up being called, "Fatso." Some years ago, in a Sunday School class at Asbury United Methodist Church (Durham, NC), where I served for eight years as a part-time associate pastor, we were talking about the power of names. I turned to a close friend and church member, and inquired, "when you were young, did they call you Bill or Billy?" My friend replied, "they mostly called me the boy in the wheelchair."

Will Willimon, former Dean of the Chapel at Duke, semi-retired United Methodist bishop, now a "mere" Divinity School professor, tells a story about a seminary retreat he led some years ago while at Duke. The point of the retreat was to help some first-year divinity students get a sense of their callings. During one of the opening exercises, Will told the students that the Holy Spirit gives every minister an intimate name, a name that expresses something about their individual calling. For example, a gifted speaker might say her name was "Preacher." A truly compassionate person might say his name was "Listener."

Will told the group that at the end of the retreat, as a closing exercise, he'd like for each of the students to stand before the group and state the special name given to him or her by the Holy Spirit. They'd have the weekend to think and pray about it. And so, during the last hour together as a retreat group, the gathering of about 15 students, along with Will, sat in a circle. One by one, the students rose, stepped into the center of the circle, and said what name they thought they'd been given by the Holy Spirit.

One young woman said she thought her name was "Comforter." Another student said, "Encourager." Will relates that things were going well until one young man stepped forward. He didn't say anything. He just silently stood there. Silence — uncomfortable silence. The group waited. More silence. Will says, "you know how uncomfortable silence makes Protestants." The silence began to express itself — in creaking furniture, students clearing their throats, glances at watches. Some students looked around, trying to determine whose turn it might be next.

Finally, the young first-year divinity student said, "I've looked for my name for three days; it just isn't there. Nothing I can think of is strong enough to undo the name I already have, the name my father gave me so many years ago. Over and over, and over, he's always told me that my name is "Not Good Enough."

> Now he was teaching in one of the synagogues on the Sabbath. And just then there appeared a woman with a spirit that had crippled her for eighteen years. She was bent over and was quite unable to stand up straight. When Jesus saw her, he called her over and said to, "Woman, you are set free from your ailment." When he laid his hands on her, immediately she stood up straight and began praising God. But the leader of the synagogue, indignant because Jesus had cured on the sabbath, kept saying to the crowd, "There are six days on which work ought to be done; come on those days and be cured, and not on the sabbath day." But the Lord answered him and said, "You hypocrites! Does not each of you on the sabbath untie his ox or his donkey from the manger, and lead it away to give it water? And ought not this woman, a daughter of Abraham whom Satan bound for

eighteen long years, be loosed from this bondage on the sabbath day?" When he said this, all his opponents were put to shame, and the entire crown was rejoicing at all the wonderful things that he was doing (Luke 13: 10–17).

The Gospel reading above — a reading found only in Luke — is about a nameless woman who encounters our Lord during a worship service. We don't know her name, but we know what people called her: she was the "bent-over" woman. She'd been bent over at the waist for 18 long years. For 18 years, she'd been unable to look anyone else in the face. For 18 years, she'd been unable to hug a child without scaring him. For 18 years, she had talked to the shoes of others. For 18 long years, others had talked to the back of her head.

Not only did the bent-over woman suffer from a disability; she was not welcome within the worship setting. Leviticus 21:18–20, referring to temple practices, states that "no one who has a blemish shall draw near, nor one who is blind, or lame, no one with a crippled foot or hand, or who is hunchbacked or dwarfed." She had to keep her distance. According to the religious law of her day, her "blemish," her condition — her infirmity — made her ritually unclean.

And, of course, almost as bad — she was a woman. In the society of that day, women were assigned to an inferior area of the temple or synagogue. Men carefully avoided them. Men particularly avoided touching — in even an "innocent" way — a woman who was outside the immediate family. What would people say? What would they think?

In the Gospel lesson noted above, Luke reminds us that Jesus, aware of society's "rules," was more concerned with society's brokenness. And so, Jesus did the unthinkable — the unlawful — the scandalous. The blemish-less Messiah, the Good Shepherd, the Lamb of God, approached the reproachable, untouchable woman, lay his hand upon her and, in doing so, healed her. If the blemish cannot approach the Lord, the Lord will approach the blemish.

Ah, Jesus healed and transformed the bent-over woman. He did so without preconditions of any kind. And everyone lived happily ever after. Of course not! For the leader of the synagogue, the transformation of the bent-over woman occurs at the wrong time. Jesus is "working" on the Sabbath — and in doing so — he's disrupting the scheduled activities of the synagogue. We see that Jesus' healing activity has caused the leader to become "bent out of shape."

It's easy for us to be critical of the religious leader. How could anyone be so heartless, so absorbed by religious concerns that he misses the chance to delight in a miracle?

Well, for one thing, the leader is like many of us. He takes the Commandments of God rather seriously. As is so often said in our "modern" context, "God didn't give Moses 'Ten Suggestions; He gave Moses Ten Commandments.'" And one of them, of course, was the Fourth Commandment:

> Remember the Sabbath day by keeping it holy. Six days you shall labor and do all your work, but the seventh day is a Sabbath to the LORD your God. On it you shall not do any work, neither you, nor your son or daughter, nor your manservant or maidservant, nor your animals, nor the alien within your gates (Exodus 20: 8–10).

From the time the Fourth Commandment was delivered to Moses, down to the time of Christ, the Hebrews had more or less perfected Sabbath observance. One knew what one could do and what one could not. For example, one could not extinguish a candle that had been lit before the beginning of the Sabbath (sundown on Friday). A fire could not be lit once the Sabbath had begun. If one was outside the Jerusalem wall, one could not carry even a handkerchief once the Sabbath started, if one wanted to avoid labor. There is some indication that if one spied a flea on one's outer garment, it could be knocked off — but not killed — on the Sabbath.

Providing Sabbath day medical care was quite a bit more nuanced. On the one hand, Hebrew law considered all life to be sacred. Efforts to preserve life did not, therefore, violate the Sabbath. But in keeping with the religious views of the time, medical treatment that could be postponed, without endangering the life of the "patient," was generally not performed until the Sabbath had ended. Considering this, we might legitimately ask ourselves the question: Just who does this Jesus think He is?

Would not the bent-over woman have been just as excited if she had been healed by Jesus one day later? She'd been bent over for 18 years; what difference was another day going to make? If we are to believe what Matthew records in chapter 5, verse 18, that Jesus came not to change one iota of the law, why didn't he just wait one more day?

The answer: well, *human* labor must stop on and for the Sabbath; God's labor does not. The rabbis of Jesus' time understood that, indeed, babies were/are born on the Sabbath, rain falls on the Sabbath — God's gift of life occurs seven days each week — not six. For Christians who view Sunday as our Sabbath, God gives life on Sundays; remember that my friend, Bunny, was even born on Easter Sunday. In His healing of the bent-over woman, Jesus is not practicing medicine; He's doing God's work. In fact, Christ is God.

In our story we see not so much what Jesus can do; we see who Jesus is. He isn't just a talented, inspiring, infectious street preacher; He is the one who comes from heaven (John 3:31). The world can no more stop Him than it can stop the coming of a new day. Wherever He is present, there is abundance and there is life. That abundance and life cannot be managed; it cannot be hemmed in. Nor can it be limited, manipulated, altered or defeated.

Jesus has healed the bent-over woman. But He's done something else: He's given her a new name. He tells the leader of the synagogue that the woman who, for 18 years has been so scorned, is a "daughter of Abraham." It's the only time in all of scripture that anyone is called by that name.

By His words and action, Jesus places a socially invisible, physically broken woman in the center of the tradition that the synagogue leader is trying to preserve. In His actions, Jesus is loudly proclaiming that God's love has a way of breaking into our routines, of forcing itself into our broken world. God is intent upon having us; He will even rename us if it suits His purposes and shows His love.

I left you hanging a while ago, didn't I? You're likely wondering what happened at the end of Will Willimon's retreat. What happened when the young man in the middle of the circle told his peers that his name was "Not Good Enough?" Will says that after the young man's revelation, there was a second period of silence. This moment of silence was even more uncomfortable than the first. Will says that it was "silence so deep you could drown in it." He adds that "there you had a group of young people who were training to become spiritual 'lifeguards' and one of their own was drowning in their midst."

But, suddenly one of the group rose from his chair, stepped into the circle, put his arms around the other young man who had been standing alone and, using the words that came from Heaven when our Lord himself was baptized said, "You are my beloved son, with whom I am well pleased" (Luke 3:21–22). Another young student, moved by the compassionate action of her classmate, stood up and joined the two in heavenly embrace. One by one, the others broke the circle and joined them as well. Amid their tears, they repeated the words to their broken comrade, "You are my beloved son, with whom I am well pleased."

Do you have a blemish? Are you bent over by the weight of sorrow, or guilt, or loss, or sin? Are there times when you look at the brokenness of your life and you say to yourself, like that young student, my name is "Not Good Enough?" Well, know this, dear friends: we *aren't* good enough. But there is Someone else who is. The blemish-less Messiah seeks us out, every one of us. He is the Good Shepherd who will not rest, Sabbath or not, until He has brought us all within the fold.

If the blemish cannot approach the Lord, the Lord will approach the blemish. He'll endure anything: the scorn and ridicule of those who are in power, the whip, the nails, the spear, even Death on a Cross, to reach out to you and to me.

Through the waters of our baptism, we drowning souls — who aren't good enough — receive a new name: "Christian." We are all heirs of the blessing. Brothers and sisters: Lift your spirits high, for we are loved by the One who gave His precious life for us all. Thanks be to God.

# 3

# Goin' to the Holy Land

"How can we know the way?"

I've always wanted to visit the Holy Land. I've always wanted to walk though Nazareth, where Jesus played as a little boy. I've dreamed of spending some time in Capernaum, where Jesus preached at the synagogue. There have been several efforts to excavate near the synagogue, to reclaim the ancient synagogue from ruins in the area along the northern coast of the Sea of Galilee. I understand that now there's a church that has been constructed on the site of what is believed to be Peter's house. It's where Jesus healed Peter's mother-in-law. I'm sure that when travelers see that spot, many come away with a special feeling — that it's Holy.

I'd love to see Bethlehem. Today, it's under Palestinian control. The Church of the Nativity is there, of course, standing in the center of the town. It's part of Manger Square. It's constructed over a grotto or cave called the Holy Crypt, where Jesus is believed to have been born. One of my dreams is to stand in that church on Christmas Eve, to breathe in all the sounds, the history, the feelings. I know that all who go there get the feeling that it is someplace special, someplace Holy.

I'd especially like to see Jerusalem, to walk the narrow winding passages that our Lord was compelled to take as he made his way, carrying his cross from Pilate's court to Golgotha. I'd relish the chance to see that *Via Dolorosa* — that way of pain. I'm sure I'd come away with a deep, abiding notion that such a place is special — it's Holy.

Goin' to the Holy Land — for much of my life, it seems, I've tried to go to the Holy Land. I've tried to journey there to that special place that is consecrated by God, to experience that treasured bit of soil where God fulfilled God's promise. That's what the Holy Land means, of course; it's the place that God has touched and in doing so, God changed it forever.

For some time now, I've begun to feel like I'll never make it. As is the case for so many of us as we grow into our later adult years, there's just so much to do and so little time to do it that I realize I'll probably never see Jerusalem. I'll probably never dip my toe into the Sea of Galilee. I'll probably never taste the waters of the River Jordan.

And yet, as I reflect upon the words of Saint John, in what we call the 14th chapter of his Gospel, I realize that I've been to the Holy Land many times. For many, many years of my life, I went to the Holy Land every time I was in the presence of my maternal grandmother — my Grandmother Lib — who died some years ago. Can you hear the promise of Jesus as given to us by the beloved apostle?

"Do not let your hearts be troubled. Believe in God, believe also in me. In my Father's house there are many dwelling places. If it were not so, would I have told you that I go to prepare a place for you? And if I go and prepare a place for you, I will come again and will take you to myself, so that where I am, there you may be also. And you know the way to the place where I am going." Thomas said to him, "Lord, we do not know where you are going. How can we know the way?" Jesus said to him, "I am the way, and the truth, and the life. No one comes to the Father except through me...."

Judas (not Iscariot) said to him, "Lord, how is it that you will reveal yourself to us, and not to the world?" Jesus answered him, "Those who love me will keep my word, and my Father will love them, and we will come to them and make our home with them (John 14: 1-6, 22-23).

Note that Jesus doesn't say that if we love him, He'll always come to us in time of troubles; no, if we love Him, and importantly, if we keep his word, Jesus won't have to come to us at all — He's *already there*, since according to John's Gospel, he's *already* "moved in." He's *already* living with us. The Lord certainly lived with Lib Grier.

Goin' to the Holy Land. If we love the Lord, and if we keep His word.... I've known lots of people in my time, but I've never known anyone who loved the Lord as much as my Grandmother Lib. Following her death some years ago, I thought it fascinating and wonderful that as we remembered the modest, soft-spoken, gentle woman, the only thing she ever did in her life to really "outdo" anyone was in the way she loved "her" Lord and kept His word? In everything else, she was always content for others to outdo her. Anyone who remembers her knows exactly what I mean.

For example, as a kid, it was never any fun to stand in a line with Grandmother Lib. That meant you were in the back, behind everyone else. At family gatherings, when my brothers and I, along with cousins Robbie, Jan, and later young Jack, spent the happiest moments of our very happy childhoods, we'd listen for Grandmother Lib's comments as the plates were filled with the Southern kitchen treasures, perfected through several generations of Crawfords and Griers. Someone would look at her plate, comment upon the small portions she'd placed there, tell her that she needed to spoon out some more for herself, and she'd say her magic words, "Oh, no, this is gracious plenty." It wasn't until years later, when Jane and I were married, and had children of our own, that I really understood what she'd meant: that joined together as family, sharing food, and talk, and laughter, and love with each other—it is, indeed, "gracious plenty."

Goin' to the Holy Land. I think I remember the first sermon I ever heard from the 14th chapter of John's Gospel. It wasn't delivered by the Reverend Anderson—the first minister that I can remember serving Olney Presbyterian Church, in Southern Gaston County, where I grew up. Nor was it either the Reverend Murray Love nor the Reverend Bill Leist, the two ministers who presided over that fine old church during most of my happy time there. No, the first sermon I likely heard from Chapter 14 of John's Gospel was delivered by the "very reverent," Elizabeth Grier. I must have been eleven or twelve. Granddaddy "Jule" had died when I was eight. We'd talked about heaven in Sunday School, so I summoned up the courage and asked my Grandmother if she thought we'd all go to heaven and if so, did she think that Granddaddy was already there?

"Certainly," she said, and as she did so, she turned and pulled her Bible open and quickly pointed to John, Chapter 14. "Let not your hearts be troubled. Believe in God, believe also in me. In my Father's house, there are many mansions …," she continued for a few more words.

I interrupted her, "but Grandmother, how do you know what it says there is true?"

Her quick retort: "These are the words of Jesus. Jesus is a gentleman; you can always take the word of a gentleman."

I was too young to realize the quiet strength that lay in those words — in my grandmother's sermon, if you will. You see, she loved the Lord. She loved the Lord with such an unquestioning faith that she could face any trial, any problem, any challenge, and know that she had all the presence that she needed. And can you understand that for my Grandmother Lib, the Lord wasn't some past-tense Messiah; He was the Present, Living Christ. You see, what my Grandmother realized, I think, is that Christ is not someone that you wait to see in heaven; no, Christ had touched her life and changed her forever; he had consecrated her and, according to his promise, *lived with her*, abided in her. In that sense, therefore, anywhere my Grandmother was, whether on Old York Road or Grissom Street, whether in the Grier Apartments or in a hospital or nursing facility, whether at Olney Church or Matthews-Belk Company, where ever she was, *there* was the Holy Land!

There are so many great stories about Miss Elizabeth, as some people called her. One story, told often by our Uncle Harold, gives us a good glimpse into Grandmother's quiet faith. It happened during the Depression years, when the economy of Gastonia was hit so hard by the closing of many of the textile mills. Times were tough, and families had to supplement their incomes in any way they could. Insurance premiums were hard to come by and so most extras — farm implements, smoke houses, and barns — were seldom insured. Behind the Grier home place was a good-sized barn that was used for all sorts of things. Late one evening, someone realized the barn was on fire. Most of the family apparently were running around trying to get water to the blaze. My mother — 93-years-old, as of this writing — was no more than seven or eight-years-old. Harold was five or so, and Jack was a toddler.

With flames licking at the roof, Grandmother must have realized that the barn was lost. The barn might be gone, but she wasn't about to give up the two-horse wagon that was still inside. As the story goes, the family turned around from their chaotic and useless efforts just in time to see Miss Elizabeth—all 110 pounds of her—pulling the heavy wagon out of the barn to safety. The next day, it was all that two or three of the men could do just to budge it. How in the world had she managed such a physical feat?

One Sunday afternoon, after "Dinner" (that's the meal right after church, for you 21st century millennials) — when Harold had told the story yet another time — we grandchildren asked Miss Lib how she'd pulled that heavy wagon. She quietly responded, "Well, I'm not sure. It didn't seem all that heavy at the time. I suppose that while I was a-pulling, the Lord must have been a-pushing."

You see, in her time of trouble, she didn't have to call on the Lord; *He was already there.* He was already there because according to the Gospel of John, He was living within her heart. She had been consecrated. Because my Grandmother loved the Lord, and kept his Word, she *was* the Holy Land.

Goin' to the Holy Land — there are just so many ways we remember my splendid Grandmother Lib. We remember that she taught Sunday School at Olney Church for almost sixty consecutive years. We remember her as the quiet ambassador at Belk's, where she managed the piece goods department for 43 years. Many described her as the fair-minded, quiet saleslady, who never tried to sell you four yards of material, if three and one-half would do.

Oh, there was certainly a serious side to Elizabeth. That side was displayed one Sunday evening more than 75 years ago. My dad and my mother were dating then. Rather than attend the Sunday evening service over at Olney, they determined that they'd prefer a picture show. I've never heard just how, but the news of their dalliance beat them home that Sunday evening. As my dad drove young Betty up the driveway, he saw Ms. Grier sweeping off a very clean front porch. My dad always said he could tell by the way she popped that broom across the planks of the front porch that the broom was really intended for him. It didn't take the broom, however; one look from my Grandmother was plenty. You didn't miss church in the Holy Land and get away with it.

Goin' to the Holy Land—The apostle John says that if you love the Lord and keep His Word, God the Father, God the Son, and God the Holy Spirit, will make God's home with you. Keeping the Lord's Word — it's easier said than done. It requires, for example, that we be concerned for others when so much of the time, we'd prefer to be concerned about ourselves.

We hear it said so often these days — "I'll pray for you" — that it can have a hollow ring. But with Elizabeth, prayer was never hollow. It was personal, it was articulate, and it was unceasing. It was local, and it was world-wide. It was often joined with the prayers of others, but it was always uniquely tied to Elizabeth's spiritual journey through this world. I wonder just how many prodigals returned to the fold in this world because of the prayers of Elizabeth? How much suffering was abated through the strength of her quiet petitions? How much sorrow was lifted up, if even just a bit, by the efforts of my Grandmother with her eyes closed? I, for one, felt an extra measure of security knowing a saint like my grandmother was praying for me every day.

Goin' to the Holy Land. If I'm right — and I know I am — every time I neared the presence of my Grandmother, I was in the Holy Land. Any time anyone else was near her, he or she was on hallowed ground.

In early December of Miss Lib's penultimate year on earth, a group of young people in Gastonia took a trip to the Holy Land. They didn't need a boat or a plane to get there. All they had to do was assemble at Courtland Terrace, a local retirement home, for some Christmas carols. I understand most had nice voices. They sang "Silent Night" for the aged and the sick. They sang "Away in a Manger," "O Little Town of Bethlehem," "It Came Upon A Midnight Clear." When it was time for them to leave, for them to retreat from that world of the aged and the infirm, to go back to the things young people like to do, one of the elderly ladies in the parlor said, "You know, it's just not Christmas without the Christmas story from Luke's Gospel. Could one of you young people read us the Christmas story?"

Well, I'm sure one or more of the youth would have been happy to do so, but for one reason or another, there was no Bible handy. They looked on the tables there and on some of the shelves and saw some various bits of reading material, but no Bible, no Gospel of Luke. And then a quiet little voice spoke up from within the group. It was my Grandmother. She'd been wheeled into the parlor by her daughter, my mother, so that she could enjoy the music.

"I know the story," rang out the quiet, yet assured words of Elizabeth. And so, all heads turned to my 95-year-old grandmother, seated in her wheelchair, as she began the wondrous story that she knew so well. "In that region there were shepherds abiding in the fields, keeping watch over their flock by night. And lo, the angel of the Lord came upon them and they were sore afraid …." By the time she had finished, there wasn't a dry eye in the room.

You see, the young folks thought they were just taking a short time out of their life to do a good deed. What they hadn't counted on, I'm sure, was an encounter with a gentle, little, 95-year old evangelizer– an evangelizer named Elizabeth. What they'd bargained for was a few minutes in a nursing home. What they got, of course, was a face-to-face encounter with one of God's special emissaries. In the wink of an eye, they'd been transported to the Holy Land since they found themselves in the presence of One who had been claimed so long ago by the Lord.

A few months later, I heard about another chorus; this time it was at Gaston Manor, a nursing home, where Grandmother had been moved. These singers were not as talented as the group of young people who'd come to Courtland Terrace at Christmas time. There wasn't anything particularly special about these folks; they were humble staff workers employed at the Manor. The 9-1-1 call had just been given, the call that would take their sweet Elizabeth to the hospital where she would spend her final hours.

There wasn't much time left. The ambulance would soon arrive. I'm sure that in each of their hearts, they knew they'd never see my Grandmother again. She was still conscious, but obviously in some difficulty. The half dozen staff people joined each other around her bed, each touching the frail, little frame of the woman who had touched so many hearts for 95 years. They sang "Amazing Grace," tears of joy rolling down their faces. You see, although these people had not known my Grandmother for very long, they had a special insight. They knew the Holy Land when they experienced it. They weren't about to give it up without some final celebration, some final worship service in which they expressed their thanks to the Lord who lived within Elizabeth, who'd chosen Elizabeth so long ago as an instrument of peace, an instrument of joy, and an instrument of love.

Goin' to the Holy Land. Miss Lib's life was such a great blessing, but we must come to understand that her life offers each of us a significant challenge. Are we willing to love the Lord and keep His word? I know my Grandmother would say, "you know, you're all such special people."

Let the Lord live in you as the Lord lived in her. Keep the word of the Lord, for you are indeed precious in His sight. And in doing so, you also will be Holy Land.

# 4

# Sioux City Christmas

"What shall I cry?"

Sometimes we are given another chance, another chance that we don't deserve, but a chance that we should eagerly grab. It may be a second bite at the apple, another swing at the pitch. We are in a bind and we welcome a chance to do something positive.

> Comfort, O comfort my people, says your God. Speak tenderly to Jerusalem, and cry to her that she has served her term, that her penalty is paid, that she has received from the Lord's hand double for all her sins. A voice cries out: "In the wilderness prepare the way of the Lord …." A voice says, "Cry out!" And I said, "What shall I cry?" (Isaiah 40: 1-2, 6a).

In this Old Testament scripture, Isaiah is talking to a people who would love another chance. The people of Judah had turned away from God, had ignored the warnings of the prophets, had incorporated their neighbors' religions into their own. These excesses had led to internal weakness and such weakness was sure to be taken advantage of by Judah's powerful neighbors. Judah had gone to war with its principal adversary, Babylon.

In its wars with Babylon, Judah had been overwhelmingly defeated. Its capital city, Jerusalem, had been captured in 597 B.C., and King Jehoiachin and his family were taken into captivity in the first Babylonian deportation described for us in II Kings. Ten years later, Judah was again locked in bitter battle with the Babylonians and this time, in 587 B.C., Jerusalem was utterly destroyed. Her walls were pulled down, the temple burned, and additional Judeans deported. For years they lived as slaves.

Isaiah's words are to a defeated people, a people held in captivity far away from home. And his words are glad tidings, welcome news, for the people are to be given another chance. In the divine speech recorded in Isaiah, God commands that comfort be proclaimed to the people. It seems the people of God have suffered enough, the years of disciplinary judgment are over, the price for the sins of the past has been paid. The end of strife and the forgiveness of sins herald a new relationship between the people and their God.

The angelic messenger in Isaiah calls for the preparation of a highway in the desert, a highway which will reveal publicly the glory of God. Yahweh's road will lead from Babylon, across the desert, back to the Promised Land. The first exodus had led the people from Egypt through the wilderness, but it had taken them forty years of heartache and trouble to find their home. This time the highway would be straight and level. It would be unobstructed.

Can you sense the feeling of hope that these words of Isaiah would have given the captives in Babylon? They had been given another chance by their God. The sins of the past were forgotten. In time they were allowed to leave. In time they returned to their homeland. In time they rebuilt Jerusalem, erected new walls, rebuilt the temple, rebuilt their lives and the lives of their children and grandchildren. In time, things returned to normal, all was right in the world.

They'd been given another chance, and, for a while, they behaved like grateful children. But after a time, when they were used to relative comfort and safety, they returned to the old ways. They forgot God's commandments. And so, they were again conquered by a neighbor. This time it was the most powerful neighbor they had ever known, Rome. Rome set up a puppet regime, with a despicable king. He ruled with cruel force. Always the people were subject to imprisonment without charge or trial.

And so, two thousand years ago the people of Judah, indeed all the people of the world, were in need of another chance — a chance which they did not deserve. Could the words of Isaiah still be true? Could God provide a highway of salvation? Would God restore the original order of the world through the gift of a Messiah or would they continue to live in strife, in slavery to their sin? Had the people messed things up so badly that there was now no hope?

It was December 1944. Unlike the mild southern winters to which the young couple had been accustomed, the Sioux City Winter had come early and with a vengeance. Cold, dreary mornings gave way to windy afternoons and bone-chilling evenings. Even on those days in which the sun marched unaccompanied by clouds across the sky, there was no respite from the cold. Married for a bit more than a year, both having been raised in rural North Carolina, the couple was not used to this bitter chill, the endless drifts of snow, nor to the feelings of loneliness and isolation in a strange world torn apart by war and desperation. Their loneliness was magnified by their knowledge that it was to be their first Christmas away from their families.

He served the war effort as one of many Army Air Corps supply corporals — cataloging, shelving, and retrieving an endless array of aircraft parts, fuel lines, ball bearings, small electric bulbs, and oil canisters. She spent her days as a clerk of a different type — surrounded by the benign inventory of one of the local five and dimes. Separately, each evening, they trudged through several blocks of snow to catch the bus to their small, off-base apartment and its meager furnishings.

It was not as if the couple lacked friends. In nearby apartments were the Kazenocecs from the plains of Indiana, the Snyders from suburban Washington, D.C., and the Morgans from Salt Lake City. Each husband an enlisted man, each wife a clerk or office worker on or near the base, the couples — friends for the better part of a year — had formed a firm bond.

The wives called the husbands the Four Musketeers and joked about how inseparable they were. In reality, they all knew they were quite separable, that with the heavy losses in the bombing raids over Europe, there was always the chance one or all of the husbands would be transferred to England to replace an American crewman shot down by a Messerschmidt or killed by German flak.

And so, notwithstanding the bond the couple felt with their newfound friends, notwithstanding the empathy shared among the small enclave, there was still a painful loneliness for the families back home. Each missed the wisdom of Mother, the silent strength of Grandmother Crawford, the warmth and charm of Granny Grier.

Sensing the couple's isolation, relatives had begun to send Christmas gifts by parcel post as early as Thanksgiving. Every few days a package would arrive and immediately the young couple would eagerly open it. The first gifts eased somewhat the feeling of separation: sweaters knitted by Aunt Ruth, some tobacco from Uncle Fouts, canned peaches from sister Aline, a five-dollar bill from sister Edith. Some later boxes contained double treats, insulated underwear — the kind that was so hard to find — wrapped in their hometown newspaper, the pages filled with news from home.

As Christmas approached, their sense of loneliness deepened as two by two, the others on the base began to travel home on furlough. The previous Christmas most of the group had been forced to stay on as the soldiers of the American theater did their part to send planes and parts to England for the planned invasion of France. The couple had been lucky, however. They had managed a Christmas pass only because the young man had performed a sort of magic, finding some scarce B-17 parts just when it seemed there were none. They had been the envy of the group last year, but this Christmas the young husband knew there was no rabbit to pull from his hat. He knew this year he'd mind his warehouse all alone. She knew she'd work at Woolworth's until 6:00 p.m. on Christmas Eve. But a box of goodies came every few days from home and the couple blocked out their sadness by tearing through the wrappings to get to the treasures lying within.

As the winter days grew shorter and shorter, the parade of presents began to subside. After the second December weekend, the postman delivered a fair sampling of holiday cards, but only a few trinkets from home. With the shortening of the days came a shortening of their tempers. The smallest thing seemed to produce a fuss. They argued over who had eaten the last of the scuppernong preserves. Who had thrown away the important part of *The Gazette*? Slamming the door one morning, the husband yelled that he couldn't understand why she'd claimed the single pair of wool socks sent by her brother Jack. "They really don't fit her," he said to himself. Inwardly he was angry that she seemed to long more for her brothers than for him.

At long last, it was Christmas Eve, but they were depressed. Nothing had been delivered for more than three days. The air base and city seemed deserted as all who could leave did so, seeking more exciting locales. It was Christmas Eve, and the sense of anticipation seemed all gone—all the Christmas cookies had been eaten, the homemade pound cake, the apple jam, the home-canned vegetables gone as well. It was Christmas Eve and with their spirits fell a new and heavy layer of snow.

As they arrived home that evening, they tried to busy themselves with the few chores required to keep up the tiny apartment. He carried the half-bag of garbage to the back alley, standing in the snow for a few minutes to gaze pensively at her silhouette on the kitchen shade. She prepared a simple supper from the few ingredients they had on hand. Neither spoke more than a few words while they ate. As they washed and dried the dishes, she suddenly excused herself so that he wouldn't see her cry. But within a few minutes, she regained her composure and suggested they listen to some music. They heard Bing Crosby dream of a White Christmas, but each silently dreamed instead of the foothills of Carolina, with its church pageants and high school football, its rolling hills and seas of yellow pine. Each longed not for sleigh bells but for the drone of the old '32 Ford pickup in which they had courted, and talked, and planned.

They gazed across their living room at the small, scraggly little tree they had decorated and realized that there was not a single present under its limbs. As if to move their thoughts from their own abject surroundings, they commented about the Christmas preparations that were no doubt already underway back home. By now the turkey was surely roasting. By now the cornbread dressing was soaking up rich broth. Granny was surely mixing the damson pudding and stirring the luscious fillings for her pies. Brothers Jack and Harold were no doubt excited about the prospects of a visit from St. Nick. Brother Boot was no doubt roasting pecans. The sounds and aroma seemed to reach out to the isolated couple over the thousand or so miles separating them from their families. The excited laughter of their furloughed friends seemed to dance over the distances as well and all this left the couple with a deep sense of longing, a deep sense of guilt and dread, since they knew their naked tree was their own doing, that the love had been sent to them from home, but that it had been consumed.

Yes, it was Christmas Eve and they were lonely. All the gifts and symbols of home and family were gone and there was nothing familiar on the Iowa landscape to ease their separation. It was Christmas Eve and the dark and empty apartments of their friends matched the feeling within their hearts. It was Christmas Eve, but for the couple, there was nothing left to celebrate. And so, with a feeling of helplessness and disappointment, they turned out the lights and went to bed, tears dampening both their pillows.

...

It must have been 7:30 or 8:00 the next morning when the pounding began — the loud pounding on the downstairs door. The young man ran down the steps to see what the problem was and there in the snow stood an unfamiliar man with an enormous box. The man nonchalantly said, "Special Delivery."

It took them both to carry the box upstairs and after they placed it on the floor, they eagerly pulled it open. Inside was a country ham, two of Mason's smoked hens, biscuits and rolls made by Mother, jelly and jam sent by Eunice, one of Janie's famous pound cakes, and all kinds of other delights. And there was a Star of David with a note attached. She could tell from the carefully formed letters that it was from her father. It said, "I know how you two are and I figured by now there'd be nothing left of the earlier packages. I've given instructions for this to be delivered Christmas morning, no matter what the expense or trouble. Know that we love you — Dad."

Another chance, another chance. They'd been given another chance. A chance to feel the warmth and love shared by family. A chance to know that they were not alone in the world, that no matter what the distance, there was a closeness that could not be broken apart.

And isn't that really what Advent is all about? Humanity has squandered the love of God, has eagerly taken what God has given, taking God and God's gifts for granted. Time after time, the heavenly Father has sent us God's love and time after time humanity has consumed it. And yet, the Christmas story prophesied in Isaiah, as told in Matthew and Luke, is a message from our Heavenly Father saying, "I know how you are and I know that there is nothing left from my earlier gifts to you, and in spite of all that, I've given special instructions that a glorious gift be delivered to you. The gift is in the form of a baby, a humble child born to a humble family. That child will show you what true power is—it's the power of love."

No expense has been spared in getting this message and gift to us. It has cost the life of a Son, God's only Son. We are special people, for in the gift of Jesus Christ, we have been given another chance.

# 5

# Begrudging Generosity

*"Are you envious because I am generous?"*

A thousand or so years ago, during the Fall of 1972, I was successful in registering for a course in Wake Forest University's Department of Religion. "American Religious Life," it was a survey course that looked at the core denominational and sectarian beliefs of the major — and some not so major — religious groups in our country. The professor was notoriously easy on college athletes, so it was a particularly popular course for those playing football or basketball. At that time in the 70s, all WFU students had to complete at least one elective in Religion in order to graduate.

The class was large by WFU standards — almost 30 students. Virtually all were athletes of one sort or another. There were only four or five "civilians" like me. One thing seemed odd: after the initial session, none of the athletes came back to class.

I did, of course. I listened carefully and took detailed notes on everything the professor said. Every afternoon, as was my habit in college, and later in law school, I read over the notes I'd taken that day and filled in a few additional points while my memory was fresh. Weeks passed without any sign of my classmates, other than the three or four of us who, like me, were dutiful in attending.

On the day of the last class before the course's final — and only — exam, I walked into a crowded classroom. All the athletic prodigals had returned. The room was full. It was as if the athletes knew some secret and I did not. A minute or so after the opening bell, the professor came into the room with a tall stack of papers that he ceremoniously plopped down on his desk.

"Here are some study guides for the final exam. *Everything* you need to know is within these pages," he said. "There is *nothing* on the exam that is not within these pages. You need not refer to our text; you need *not* refer to your own notes, for *here is everything* you need."

He paused for a second or two, looked around the room, and said, "Mr. Robinson, will you and Mr. Jerrod (not his real name) see that everyone in the class gets a copy of these study guides?"

Was it the redness in my face? Was it the steam that seemed to be escaping from my ears and nostrils? I had given out perhaps three or four copies to a few athletes near me when I heard the following from the professor: "I have a question for Mr. Robinson."

Startled, I turned to face the professor. He said, "Mr. Robinson, do you begrudge my generosity?" (see Matt. 20:15 for the similarly worded question, "Are you envious because I am generous?").

I thought to myself, "Is the Pope Catholic?" Yet I stammered a quick, "Errr. No sir."

He then retorted — with a bit of a twinkle in his eye, I'll add — "Class, Mr. Robinson has just seen a recapitulation of the parable of the workers in the vineyard (*see* Matt. 20:1-16). I trust that he, and you, will someday come to understand the meaning and power of Grace."

# 6

# A Few Harsh Words

"Eloi, Eloi, lema sabachthani?"

He walked down the corridor of the VA hospital toward Bill's room. He wondered what sort of talk they'd have today. For several years they had enjoyed countless and fine conversations about all sorts of subjects. You see, like the visitor, Bill was an avid reader and the two would sometimes discuss literature or philosophy. Inevitably, however, no matter what the context of their conversation or common reading, the talk would turn to issues of faith, a discussion of the journey of faith that each had experienced.

As the visitor stuck his head into the hospital room, expecting to find Bill reading or napping, he was taken aback by the horrible expression on his friend's face. The pain was so intense that Bill's breathing was shallow, as if the very air in the room was fire, its intake adding to the flames of the infection within. Bill managed a faint smile and, and without so much as a greeting, immediately whispered, "Read me a Psalm, read me a Psalm."

From the general circumstances and the specific words, the visitor knew that this conversation was to take the form of a pastoral call, and so he assumed that uneasy position and quietly said, "Glad to, Bill, how 'bout the 23rd?"

Bill grimaced, "No thanks, I'm not in a 23rd mood, read me the 22nd or perhaps the 31st."

Though a graduate of Duke's Divinity School, the visitor didn't consider himself an Old Testament scholar. He did think the 22nd Psalm was not really appropriate for someone like Bill, in desperate pain and on his last leg. After all, that's the Psalm that begins with the words "My God, My God, why hast thou forsaken me?"

And so, the pastor turned to the unfamiliar 31st. He was doing just fine until he came to the verse that we number 10:

> For my life is spent with sorrow, and my years with sighing; my strength fails because of my misery, and my bones waste away. I am the scorn of all my adversaries, a horror to my neighbors, an object of dread to my acquaintances; those who see me in the street flee from me. I have passed out of mind like one who is dead; I have become like a broken vessel. For I hear the whispering of many—terror all around!—as they scheme together against me (Ps. 31:10-13).

Bill's visitor became uncomfortable, stopped and quickly said, "Bill, don't you think you ought not to complain to God, that instead you ought to be thinking positive thoughts, looking on the bright side?"

And in his wonderfully earthy manner, Bill said to his friend, "Tom, today there is no bright side. I hurt like the dickens, and I'm sick of this pain. I think God's up to a few harsh words, don't you? What's he goin' to do — stop loving me?"

Fact is, most of us are quite comfortable with the happy Psalms: number 23, "The Lord is my Shepherd"; number 46, "God is our refuge and strength, a very present help in trouble"; or number 48, "Great is the Lord, and greatly to be praised." We are a bit uneasy with the Psalms of Lament, these Psalms of Darkness. The power of positive thinking has become such a watchword in our society that most of us shy away from those portions of scripture that admit that the world around us is not always rosy. Anything less than overabundant optimism brands us a sniveling, weak-kneed, whiner.

We may be quite comfortable with prayers of petition. "Lord, give me power to face the challenges ahead." Or "Lord, give me inner strength to bear great pain or loss." We have been taught that it's ok to ask for something from God, so long as it is not just a selfish request for material resources.

We have been taught there is something wonderful and Stoic about bearing up to great pain or sorrow without whimpering and we, therefore, look upon prayers of petition as being acceptable. But many of us are also taught that a prayer of complaint — pure and utter complaint — would not be fitting for a Believer, someone who has been born anew by water and the Spirit.

And yet, if one reads about the children of Israel, through their history of ups and downs, freedom and captivity, plenty and want, happiness and suffering, one is left with the understanding that this people, marked as special by God, were not only rich in their language of praise and thanksgiving, but vivid in their language of sorrow and sadness. Not only were they able to stand on the mountaintop and shout praises to God Almighty, but they were able to struggle through the valleys and cry out to the one force that had always sustained them. They were not burdened by our "modern" notions of Stoic resignation to sadness. They understood what Bill was to later understand, that God was up to a few harsh words. After all, what was God going to do, stop loving them?

And although it may make us uncomfortable, we have to admit that Jesus himself was completely at ease uttering the Psalms of Darkness. We may think it is one thing for us, the weak-kneed, whimperers to fall short of the ideal, but Jesus never would have allowed himself to fail so miserably.

And yet, as Jesus entered Jerusalem looking on the people who would claim him as an earthly king, but not as a suffering servant, was not sadness in his eye? As he contemplated the betrayal by Judas, the denial by Peter, the abandonment by the others, did not he think about the words of the 31st Psalm? "I have become a reproach, especially to my neighbors, and an object of dread to my acquaintances" (Ps. 31:11). As he contemplated the chief priests and the Sanhedrin, did he not surely think of the words, "While they took counsel together against me, they schemed to take away my life" (Ps. 31:13)?

And as they nailed him to the splintered cross, did not he say, "Eloi, Eloi, lema sabachthani?"(which means, "My God, My God, Why Hast Thou Forsaken Me?" (Mark 15:34)). You see, Jesus knew — Jesus knows — what Bill was to come to understand, that God is up to a few harsh words. After all, what was God going to do with Jesus, stop loving him?

The Psalms of darkness may be understood by the secular world as acts of unfaith and failure, but for the trusting community, for the true church, their use is an act of ultimate faith. It is an act of faith which insists that the world around us must be experienced not with rose colored lenses, but as it really is. We need not pretend that this world is ordered and sane, when often it is not. We need not go through our lives whistling in the darkness. Uttering a Psalm of darkness is not an exercise in pessimism, but rather a positive statement to the world around us that all experiences of life, not just the good, *but especially the bad*, are subjects for conversation with God.

God is not some tottering old man, a sick patient from whom we must hide the diagnosis. God is our Creator. God is our Master, God is the very essence of our lives. To withhold our sorrow and our sadness from God is an act of supreme arrogance, for in doing so we withhold part of our lives from the sovereignty of God.

The Psalms of darkness become important to us because they teach us that we must verbalize not just the times of joy, the times of laughter and warmth, but we must also verbalize the times of true and deep sorrow and sadness. *Everything* must be taken to the Lord in conversation.

In a world that attempts to have us believe that given enough human power, enough human wisdom, enough human effort, all the terror can be tamed, all the darkness can be banished, our experience tells us that the nature of terror and darkness is resilience. The Psalms of darkness, repeated as they are by Jesus himself during the week of Passion, teach us that the God we worship is not a God who needs protection from our cries of pain and suffering. Ironically, the act of unbelief turns out to be committed by those who refuse to address God in their pain, thinking that God just might not be up to the confrontation.

God is up to the confrontation. The Psalms of darkness show us that it is alright to admit to ourselves and to our God that sometimes we're not in "a 23rd mood." Some days there is no bright side. We need not look at the death of a child, the death of a spouse, an unexplained illness or disease, the loss of relationship with another person, or any other example of true human pain and sorrow and try to explain it away in terms of goodness.

God is not some dummy. Don't we think that God knows the world is chaotic and broken? We are never to shut God out. If the world has beaten us down, if it has given us a crown of human thorns, if circumstances are just beyond our own understanding and control, even if we are about to be nailed to the cross that Christ would have us all bear for one another, we must not shut God out — the God who would share our sadness.

Do you ever stare at a photograph ... through tears? Do you ever think about a relationship and wonder where in the world did it go wrong? If the Gospel story tells us anything, it tells us to reach out steadfastly to God, even in our times of sorrow — especially in our times of sorrow. We are not to inflict harsh words upon those around us, but our Faith; yes, brothers and sisters, our Faith, teaches us that God is up to a few harsh words.

After all, what's God going to do, stop loving us? Of course, not.

# 7

# Love is a Verb!

"Do you love me when it's dark?"

In Paul's first letter to the church at Corinth, he offers his oft-quoted words regarding the wisdom of children:

> When I was a child, I spoke like a child, I thought like a child, I reasoned like a child; when I became an adult, I put an end to childish ways (1 Cor. 13:11).

Notwithstanding the wisdom of the Apostle Paul, it has been my experience that sometimes the most profound questions and expressions of faith can come from the mouths of children, even four-year-olds. Take our youngest, Gray, when he was four. He's now is 32; he and April have a four-year-old, and a three-year-old (and one on the way) — of their own.

I recall one specific evening many years ago, when it was my turn to put Gray to bed. I recall that he was in a particularly cooperative and agreeable mood. He'd given me no trouble that evening as I told him it was time for bed. His general attitude had put me in a warm and affectionate mood.

Gray finished his prayers, blessed all his toys and stuffed animals, and leaned back in his bed. I hugged him a few times. Kids often give concrete answers to abstract questions and, knowing exactly what his answer would be, I said, "Gray, how much do you love me?"

In his typical fashion at that time, he said "five."

I hugged him again and said, "I love you so much."

And then, from out of the blue, Gray said, "Do you love me when it's dark?"

His question caught me completely off guard and my response was something like, "Of course, of course, I love you when it's dark. I love you all the time. I love you when it's light; I love you when it's dark. What makes you ask if I love you when it's dark?"

"Well, I can't see you when it's dark," he said.

I wandered off downstairs, scratching my head, chuckling to myself about the crazy mind of a four-year-old. It was only later, after several months of thinking about his question, after reading the 5th chapter of Matthew several times, that I finally had a sense of what Gray was actually talking about.

> You are the light of the world .... In the same way, let your light shine before others, so that they may see your good works and give glory to your Father in heaven (Matt. 5:14, 16).

"Can they see us when it's dark?" Perhaps one of the problems with the *visibility* of our love is the fact that all too often, when we say the words, "I love you," we are primarily describing the "feeling" that we have in our hearts for another person. While that feeling is important, perhaps even vital to our well-being, four-year-old Gray's question, and the words of St. Matthew, have a completely different emphasis. Yes, it may truly be that love is a feeling, but in truth, we must come to discover that love is really a response. Love is not so much something to be felt, but rather, it is something to be acted out. In other words, the *love* that Christ was talking about isn't so much a noun; it's a verb.

"Can they see us when it's dark?" You see, if love is primarily a feeling within me, four-year-old Gray — or now, his four-year-old, Maggie — cannot see my love when it is dark, because the darkness hides my facial expression. If my love is primarily a feeling, the child — or anyone else, for that matter — can be left with the idea that my love is here one minute, when the conditions are right, when times are good, and gone the next, for darkness can hide my very presence. It is only when my love is expressed not merely as a feeling, but as an action, that Gray, or anyone else, can truly see the constancy of such love.

"Can they see us when it's dark?" Whenever I counsel a couple to be married, I love to ask them a trick question: "How many times during the wedding ceremony is the groom asked *if* he loves the bride?"

The answer, of course, is *zero*! During a wedding ceremony, while it is fair to say that the couple's existing love is important — without it the couple wouldn't be present for the ceremony at all — the real emphasis in a Christian wedding relates to future *actions* of such love.

It is often easy to answer the question, "Do you love someone?" It is another matter, altogether, to respond to the question, "Will you love that someone?" Love in the present tense can be described very well in terms of feelings, but love in the future sense, the sense described in wedding vows, is an active kind of experience.

43

That sort of love — the active variety — has an awesome power, according to the words of Jesus. It has the power not only to transform a relationship between two people, but the power to change the lives of others who witness it. The sort of love that Jesus is describing, through the scripture given to us by St. Matthew, is like a city set on a hill commanding the landscape, a source of hope and inspiration for all who can see it (Matt. 5:14b-15).

That sort of love — love as a verb and not merely as a noun — cannot be held within; it must be acted out, put on public display. It is daring and optimistic. It claims a power to transform and effect even when the forces at work against it are powerful and may seem overwhelming. The sort of love that Jesus is describing, when echoed throughout our lives and put on public display, can be like a pinch of salt, which seems insignificant when viewed against the cups of flour needed to bake a loaf, but which is vital in giving flavor and seasoning to that bread.

"Can they see us when it's dark?" The love described by Jesus — and Paul — is not a love that is confined to marriage. Indeed, therein lies Love's true power. For the doctrine of love that Jesus commands is not limited to our households; it is not a description of relationship just between parent and child, between husband and wife. It is a divine command that applies to us all as we interact with one another. We are *all* called upon to examples of Christ's love. We can *all* be lamps which dispel the darkness.

"Can they see us when it's dark?"

# 8

# It's All in the Voice

"How long will you keep us in suspense? If you are the Messiah, tell us plainly."

In many respects, the story of Jesus, particularly as detailed by the apostle John, is a steady journey from Galilee toward Jerusalem, a movement from the relative safety of small-town Palestine to the dangers inherent within the "sophisticated" capital city, Jerusalem. It is a sojourn from the relative obscurity of life as a carpenter's son to a very public death on the Cross. Jesus does not travel alone, of course; he is accompanied by a band of apostles. They were drawn to Jesus by his charisma, his quiet, yet immense power, his wisdom, and his resolve. No doubt they sensed that they were all involved in an adventurous enterprise that was larger than life.

As we read John's gospel, we see that Jesus is slowly constructing an identity mosaic. Knowing that the Hebrews expect a particular kind of Messiah, Jesus is determined that they come to understand that His true nature cannot be viewed with such short-sighted lenses. He has not come just to reclaim Israel; He has come to reclaim the world.

Ignoring, for the moment, the many miracles described in the Synoptic gospels, we see that by the time we get to chapter 10 of John's gospel, Jesus has performed some impressive "signs" (John's word for Jesus' miracles). He has turned water into wine (John 2), healed the child of a royal official (John 4), healed a man who has been an invalid for 38 years (John 5), fed 5,000 people with meager resources (John 6), walked on water (John 6) ,and given sight to the man who had been blind since birth (John 9).

This last sign — the healing of the man blinded from birth — is particularly impressive. No such miracle had ever been performed at any point depicted in the Hebrew Bible, "our" Old Testament. All the aforementioned signs make particularly ironic the question that is put to Jesus by the religious leaders in what has come down to us as the tenth chapter of John: "How long will you keep us in suspense? If you are the Messiah, tell us plainly" (John 10: 24b).

As the younger generations today would say, "Duh!"

What does Jesus have to do or say to convince these leaders? In wonderful irony, John's story shows us that the man who was blinded from birth now sees, while the ones who are in charge of theology are totally blind to the conditions and circumstances around them. Indeed, none are so blind as those who refuse to see. Jesus adds that the works He has done in His Father's name bear witness to His identity. He continues with a powerful indictment — "You don't believe, because you do not belong to my sheep" (John 10:26).

Earlier in this chapter, we have seen Jesus use the metaphor of shepherd and sheep to describe the relationship between himself and his following: "I am the good shepherd. The good shepherd lays down his life for the sheep" (John 10:11).

Expanding upon the metaphor that would have been so familiar to people within that agrarian community, Jesus continues: "My sheep hear my voice. I know them, and they follow me. I give them eternal life, and they will never perish" (John 10:27-20).

*Vox Christi* — the voice of Christ — the Church has always understood it to have great power. We saw that the voice of Christ, as He uttered the name, "Mary," on Easter morning, was enough to convince Mary Magdalene that Christ had indeed been raised from the dead. Later that day, it was sufficient to burn the hearts of the two who walked toward Emmaus. On that first Easter evening, the Messiah's voice stilled the fears of the apostles who had assembled in relative paralysis after the death of their Master.

One week later, the *Vox Christi* was all that it took to turn the "doubting" Thomas into a stalwart post-Easter advocate for the early church. Still later — but before His ascension — the voice of Christ was all that was necessary to grant Peter forgiveness for his three-fold denial. It was also sufficient to challenge Peter to feed Christ's sheep.

Indeed, the voice of Christ is understood to be so wonderful and powerful that reference to it is made by Roman Catholics just before approaching the altar for Holy Communion. Using the words of the centurion, they pray:

> Lord, I am not worthy that you should enter under my roof, but only say the word and my soul shall be healed (*see* Matt. 8:8).

The soothing, comforting voice of Christ still resounds in our world. From time to time over these many years since our time at Asbury UMC, here in Durham, I have shared stories about a young mother and father who, along with the entire Asbury community, lost a beloved young daughter to brain cancer more than 25 years ago. Some of you who read this may have been intimately bound up within the life and death of that little saint, Jennifer Auman.

Jennifer spent a significant part of the last year of her five-year life in Duke University Medical Center. During one such hospitalization, it was my turn as Asbury's Associate Pastor to make the Saturday morning visits to Duke. Yet, as I entered little Jennifer's room in the children's cancer wing, I saw Wally Ellis, the senior pastor at Asbury, was already there. He was standing beside her bed, holding the little girl's hand. Thinking that he had absentmindedly forgotten that he'd given me the Saturday duties that morning, I said, "Wally, I thought you wanted me to check on our folks today."

He turned to me and smiled, "That's right, you check on the others; I just came to see my little buddy." The level of affection between the two was obvious for everyone to see.

By this point in the medical process, the combination of the cancer and the efforts to rid the child's body of it had taken their toll. Still, Jennifer never complained, no matter how many times she was stuck, no matter how sick the prophylactic cocktail dripping into her arm made her, she sweetly went on. That Saturday morning, we made some idle talk for a minute or two and then Jennifer turned to Wally and excitedly said, "Wally, guess who came to see me early, early this morning?"

Wally said, "Who?"

"Jesus!"

Wally smiled, patted her little hand, and said, "Jennifer, how do you know it was Jesus?"

Jennifer looked at Wally and, without hesitation, said, "Oh, silly — I can always tell by his voice."

# 9

# The Bread Line

"How can this man give us his flesh to eat?"

As many of you know, for almost nine years *during* my long Duke University vocational tenure, I was also privileged to serve as a part-time local pastor at Asbury United Methodist Church, adjacent to Duke's East campus. On any Methodist "demographic" list, Asbury would not, however, have been described as a "campus church;" it was (and still is) "an aging congregation."

As you may also know, following in the Wesleyan traditions, Methodists take Holy Communion in several manners. Particularly for Methodists in the South, the "preferred" method is for the congregation to proceed to the altar area in groups, with the congregants kneeling — if able to do so. There they receive the elements and then are dispatched back to the pews with some appropriate words of blessing from the minister. It's a marvelous, poignant, spiritual method of celebrating the Eucharist. It can, however, be slow, particularly for a congregation filled with senior citizens. All that kneeling and rising can be problematic. Worse, it can extend the worship service past the required dismissal at noon, placing the church members at the back of the all-important line at the local cafeteria for the special Sunday buffet.

The senior pastor at the time came to me one day and said, "Tom, we have to speed Communion up. I'm getting some complaints from the Administrative Board. Got any ideas?"

> The Jews then disputed among themselves, saying "How can this man give us his flesh to eat?"
> So Jesus said to them, "Very truly I tell you, unless you eat the flesh of the Son of Man and drink his blood, you have no life in you. Those who eat my flesh and drink my blood have eternal life, and I will raise them up on the last day; for my flesh is true food and my blood is true drink" (John 6:52-55).

Knowing that the folks over at Duke University Chapel could read four scriptures, sing three hymns, have two special presentations by its glorious choir, hear an engaging twenty-minute sermon, serve Holy Communion to a thousand souls, and still get out in an hour, I suggested that we should try Communion by intinction. "It'll speed things up," I said. At the next Board meeting, the senior pastor mentioned that we were going to try to speed things up a bit and that the intinction plan was "Tom's idea."

Following our first Eucharistic observance under the "new" procedure, I had an unannounced visitor during my Tuesday afternoon office hours. It was one of the older gentlemen in the congregation; he was actually one of my favorites. I asked him what brought him by and he said he wanted to talk to me about the "new" Communion method. Thinking I'd be complemented for the speed with which we had dispensed our Lord's Body and Blood two days earlier, I said "Sure."

"Well, I don't like it," the gentleman began. "Reminds me of a bread line. Tom, I was a teenager during the Depression and things got so bad here in Durham that at one point my family had to go to the bread line, and I swore if I ever got out of that Depression, I'd never stand around, line up, and shuffle forward to receive anything to eat again. I ain't going to start now."

I had no reply. He'd already mentioned the matter to the senior pastor and, as you can imagine, when it came time for Holy Communion again, we went back to "tradition."

A year or so later, I looked at the preaching schedule and realized that I'd be in Asbury's pulpit for the Third Sunday in Lent (that year was a "C" in Lectionary terms). I thought about bread lines when I read over the Old Testament reading for the week.

> Ho, everyone who thirsts, come to the waters; and you that have no money, come, buy and eat! Come, buy wine and milk without money and without price (Isaiah 55:1).

Isaiah, of course, wasn't speaking to "modern" American Christians. His audience was a group of exiled Hebrews in Babylon. But he realized the importance of food and its power to hold together a group who had been displaced far from their homeland. "Hear my words," the prophet was saying, and you will be richly fed by the renewal of the covenantal blessing. Isaiah reminded his people that *who* fed them was of great importance. They could eat with the Babylonians and lose their identify or they could "feast" with their fellow Israelites (even though outward appearances might indicate that the food offered by the prophet was quite modest) and continue their Communion with God.

Centuries later, a wanderer named Jesus of Nazareth would say, "I am the bread of life. He [or she] who comes to me will never go hungry, and he [or she] who believes in me will never be thirsty" (John 6:35). He would add that it is in the consumption of Jesus Christ that we experience eternal life.

Someone like me — who has never been hungry, who has never been without — should be reluctant to think too harshly about my proud friend and his reluctance to shuffle forward in a line to receive a morsel of bread. Can we see, however, that in at least one important manner, my friend was absolutely right? Holy Communion, The Lord's Supper, Eucharist — however it is known in your congregation — *is a bread line.*

When it comes to being able to purchase what's being served, we are without currency. In that real sense, we who receive the elements are recipients of true charity. Those of us who are too proud to take charity will always have difficulty understanding why someone like Jesus, who had no sin of His own, bore our sin and was willing to suffer Death, even Death on the Cross, in order that we — who don't deserve it — might live.

Don't be afraid. Let's get in the Bread Line.

# 10

# The Sunday Buffet[1]

"Hungry?"

The centurion replied, "Lord, I do not deserve to have you come under my roof. But just say the word, and my servant will be healed (Matt. 8:8).

Quietly, the sojourner stood at his pew,
Softly repeating the familiar words:
"It is right and good to give our thanks and praise."
His eyes glistened as he joined the heavenly company in its unending
    hymn:
"Holy, holy, holy Lord, God of power and might, ...."
Blessed is He who comes in the name of the Lord."


He listened to the reminder of the mighty acts of Christ,
Silently wondering, "How strange is this upside-down Gospel,

---

1   Copyright 2002. Thomas A. Robinson. All rights reserved.

## Thomas A. Robinson

Its wisdom counted as folly by most all the world.
How marvelously out of synch Its standards,
The last placed first, gaining life by losing it,
Could strength, indeed, be found within weakness?"


For half a century he'd sought after the Lord,
First as an infant, then as a lad and student,
Finally, as a father, teacher and scholar, he'd made it his quest.
In the manner of the wise triumvirate who brought gold, frankincense
    and myrrh,
This wanderer had always brought his finest gifts to lay upon the altar:
Time, service, commitment—and yet his yearning went unfulfilled.


Deceptively simple—this wine, these few pieces of bread,
And yet, breaking the Body for someone like him,
Sacrificing the Righteous—that the sinful might live—it was but one
    more contradiction.
The eager line steadily moved forward until his turn it was.
Into the cup he dipped the Corpus Christi and lifted it to his
    waiting lips.
The Bread sought out his hunger and he was filled.

# 11

# It's Lunch Time!

*"Have you ever tasted Woolworth's food?"*

One of my many mentors, the Reverend Wallace Kirby, often talked about the blessings of serendipity. It's a word most of us don't use very often, but as you know, it means the process of coming to a wonderful discovery totally by accident.

Much of what we learn or experience in this world comes about through careful planning and diligent work. It has been my experience, however, that it is through serendipity — those marvelous, unexpected discoveries that we "trip over" in our lives — that we often gain so much more. My life has been richly blessed with moments of such serendipity.

I vividly recall one such moment that occurred while I worked at the Matthews-Belk store in downtown Gastonia during the middle of the turbulent sixties. "The Store," as we called it, occupied a place of high importance in my family. Our Dad was an executive both there and in the Belk headquarters in Charlotte for more than twenty-five years. My maternal grandmother worked there in piece goods for almost forty-five years. And, as my three brothers and I still joke, the four of us worked in every department in "the Store" at one time or another, with the exception of ladies' lingerie. There was so much to learn in those days and the store provided such a splendid education, but usually we received those lessons in unexpected moments.

It was in the summer of our sixteenth year that my twin brother, Todd, and I "broke through the race barrier" and became the first white porters at the Store. Porters were required to do everything no one else would do, from carrying out trash, to cleaning bathrooms, to mopping sales floors — all hard and menial labor. Because of the lowly duties, the job of porter in those days was reserved only for young black men.

> There is no longer Jew or Greek, there is no longer slave or free, there is no longer male and female; for all of you are one in Christ Jesus (Gal. 3:28).

Todd and I knew the work was filthy and difficult and that we would have to report to the store each day by 6:30 a.m., but we talked Dad into making the facilities manager hire us as porters for part of that the summer since we had an ulterior motive. Going to work so early also meant we we'd be dismissed at 2:30 p.m., giving us most of the afternoon — and all evening — to pursue other, more "important" ventures.

When you go to work that early, you eat lunch in the middle of the morning, long before the sales people do. After all, they have only been on duty little more than an hour when it's the middle of the porter's workday. Eating lunch that summer was a new and unique experience, not just because of the time of day, but because of the company; we ate with the other porters and sometimes three or four older black women — the ladies who operated the store's elevators.

One morning we were all sitting around in part of the warehouse, opening up our lunch. The other porters had been kidding Todd and me all morning, poking good natured fun at us because we were the only white guys ever to wear the grey porter's uniform, talking about how far the civil rights movement had come for us to be *allowed* to work with them. Our talk drew a bit more serious as we began to discuss black and white relations, the school consolidation that had just taken place in Gastonia, with the resulting closing of the old "colored" high school, and about whether blacks ought to be allowed to see movies in the two downtown movie houses.

I think it was probably me, not Todd, who said that a person shouldn't be forced to share his business with people with whom he wasn't comfortable. And it was certainly one of them who said, "Well look at all of us, we ain't real comfortable havin' you eat with us, but you're here anyhow, and nobody had to get arrested at any sit-in to give you the right to eat that sandwich."

After his well-put sentence, my thoughts trailed away a bit, to a dime store in Greensboro that I'd never seen, but had heard about, how a few years earlier a few black college students had refused to leave a lunch counter until they were served, how they'd been arrested, and how important that act of peaceful defiance had been in opening up shops, restaurants, and even bathrooms to blacks here in the South.

I heard the naive, rather stupid, words pour forth from my mouth, "Why did they choose the Greensboro Woolworths? Have you ever tasted Woolworth's food?"

And then came the serendipity.... From off to the right I heard the gentle, yet firm, voice of a woman who had been left out all her life. She said, "Child, you're missing the point. We're not talkin' 'bout food. We're talkin' about community, about who is included, and who is always *excluded*."

I'm sure my face reddened in embarrassment. In my sheltered immaturity, I had failed to see the tremendous symbolism of the lunch counter, that rich or poor, black or white, male or female, strong or weak, we can never be brothers and sisters until we are able to sit and eat a simple meal together.

We can share ideas. We can share funny stories. We can share common histories, but if you won't eat the simple meal with me, we will never be able to share in community with each other.

That's one of the important reasons we share the simple meal that is before us each Sunday on the Lord's Table. We share and pray for a day when the hatred and bitterness in this world will be overcome by the Love and Joy that is ours as brothers and sisters in Christ.

# 12

# A Favorable Time

"Is it because of September 11?"

My most vivid recollection of the years I spent at Huss High School — Jane went to rival Ashley High, so she doesn't figure into the "vivid" equation here — is of a particular U.S. History class in April of my Junior year (1968). The teacher, Ron Hardman, was head wrestling coach and a social studies instructor. Some would have argued that Hardman was more coach than teacher; any such characterization would have cut him to the quick.

I don't remember his lectures at all; fifty years can do that, you know. I don't remember his quizzes, any papers he assigned, nor any specific topics we discussed en masse. I do remember his passion. Those of us on the basketball team could sometimes hear his fervent pronouncements to the wrestlers, with whom we shared the gym. He'd preach about a wrestler's personal commitment, about the power of the human will, about how sheer drive and determination could often overcome a lack of speed, or skill, or strength. He was a pugilistic evangelist of sorts and the passion of his talk raised not a few eyebrows. Yet, he was even more passionate about History.

Since United States History was a required course for all North Carolina's high school students in those days, we had all sorts of kids in the class. Some, like me, were actually destined to major in History in college. Others were there only to get a ticket punched; their plans after high school — if they finished high school at all — included anything but an awareness of the Gettysburg Address, the Great Depression, or the Articles of Confederation.

Hardman didn't seem to mind the mixed bag of students. He did his best to interest us all. He tried to make the nation's history come alive. Most days History failed to cooperate, or rather, most days we students failed to cooperate. On a few days, however, I could tell that his message really clicked, that it came through even to those in the class who weren't used to listening, those who just watched the slow progress of the minute hand in the big classroom clock over Mr. Hardman's head.

As first period began on Friday morning, April 5, 1968, Hardman was already the talk of the school.

"He's been here making posters since 2:00 a.m.," whispered the school secretary, wife of the baseball coach.

"Ron's gonna pop a vein," uttered one of the assistant principals.

"I called his wife; she said leave him alone; he just has to work through this," related one of the other social studies teachers.

When it was time for my third period History class to begin, I wandered upstairs, walked into the room, and immediately realized why everyone was so alarmed. The entire atmosphere within the classroom was eerie. The rostrum, from which Mr. Hardman taught daily, was draped in black. Two entire walls made up a gigantic collage of photographs of the Reverend Dr. Martin Luther King, Jr. The words: "I have a dream!" were stenciled carefully onto the blackboard with red chalk. Mr. Hardman had set up a reel-to-reel tape recorder in the back of the classroom; it's speakers blaring one of the several sermons of Dr. King. I looked at the familiar bank of push-out windows along the outside wall and saw Mr. Hardman had stretched out a five-foot paper banner at an odd, forty-five-degree angle, its words printed in his familiar serifed, block-like alphabet:

> Proclaim the message; be persistent whether the time is favorable or unfavorable; convince, rebuke, and encourage, with the utmost patience in teaching.

Emboldened and displayed on the bias, the words were haunting and powerful. The admonition contained no attribution to the author, St. Paul. Being no scholar of scripture at the time, I had no idea the quote was from the New Testament (2 Tim. 4:2b). I supposed the words had been originally uttered by the black civil rights leader whose photos now adorned the walls of our class. I assumed the words were some sort of rallying cry, some siren-like slogan coined by the controversial preacher who'd traveled around the nation with his messages of nonviolent protest, the young Negro leader who'd been slain the prior evening outside a Memphis, Tennessee motel room.

Mr. Hardman had made no secret of the high regard that he held for the Nobel laureate from Alabama, the gentle man whom so many in the South and elsewhere seemed to hate. Hardman was one of only a handful of Caucasian men I knew at the time who'd openly praised the civil rights leader. On two or three occasions, Hardman had assigned some of Dr. King's writings. In Hardman's brusque, yet passionate manner, he'd tried to tell us about the good that could come from those who would not return evil with evil, who'd soak up hatred like a fresh sponge and give back only love in return. A lot of good King's ideas had done, many of us thought—they'd gotten him killed.

And so, on April 5, 1968, Hardman's hero was dead. Some were cheering that demise; others cried the bitter tears of seeming defeat. For someone like Hardman, whose leader and dreams had been shattered by an assassin's bullet, it was an unfavorable time—an absolutely unfavorable time.

And yet, in the early hours of that morning, Hardman had risen from his bed when he could not sleep. He'd gathered his collection of photos, taped messages, speeches, newspaper clippings and the like, and he'd gone to the place where he was most comfortable—the classroom in upstairs "B" Hall at Hunter Huss. He'd made careful preparations for his history classes that Friday. All day long, in the face of his pain and grief, he'd told the story of Dr. King. And some of us — at least one of us — listened.

Before that day, there had been a part of me that had agreed with the others who thought Hardman was a kook, but there had always been another part of me that had been attracted to the message that could stir such passion in someone like Hardman. And so, that "other part" of me listened carefully that blue April Friday as Mr. Hardman played portions of Dr. King's famous speeches and as he read his hastily prepared biography of the slain Southern leader. That other part listened as I heard Hardman relate his fears that Dr. King's murder would lead to all sorts of reactive backlashes, that there'd no doubt be riots, lootings, burnings in many of America's cities. As I say, our class that day was an unforgettable experience for me.

Two years later, when I visited my high school alma mater during Fall break of my freshman year at Wake Forest, I happened to run into Mr. Hardman in the hallway at Huss. He asked how things were going. We exchanged some small talk for two or three minutes before I blurted out the question: "What was with the banner over the windows the day after Dr. King was killed? What did all that mean?"

"It was the lowest day of my life," Hardman replied. "It was as if everything I ever believed was struck down by the sniper's bullet. As I went to bed that night, as I lay there tossing and turning, wondering how the world would ever go on without Dr. King, some words of a speech I'd once heard him give kept haunting my brain. It was a speech he'd given to a bunch of teachers at a rally, years before. He said, 'I solemnly urge you: proclaim the message: be persistent whether the time is favorable or unfavorable; convince, rebuke, and encourage, with the utmost patience in teaching.'"

"That's right," I nervously replied. "Those were the words on your banner."

"Since the evening I first heard that speech," Mr. Hardman retorted, "those have *always* been the words on my banner. You see, it was as if Dr. King was talking to me that night, saying it didn't matter if times were good or times were bad, it didn't matter if people listened or if they ignored me, my job was to persevere, my duty was to continue on in my efforts as a teacher, to convince and encourage, and even sometimes to rebuke, but always to be patient in my teaching. And so, as I lay there in my bed the night he was killed, I realized that as unfavorable as the time might be, there was but one thing for me to do and that was to get up, go to school, prepare for the next class — to persevere."

I wish I'd thought of Ron Hardman and the 2 Timothy passage years later when, on September 11, 2001, I saw replay after replay after replay of the jetliner crashing into the side of the World Trade Tower. I didn't, you know. Instead, my first thoughts were something along the lines of St. Luke's Gospel: "As for these things that you see, the days will come when not one stone will be left upon another, all will be thrown down" (Luke 21:6). I wish I'd remembered Hardman's banner and its noble message.

I wish we'd all had Mr. Hardman's 1967-68 History class, that we all remembered that crazy, weird, special class on Friday, April 5, 1968, about the power in absorbing evil without lashing back with more evil. We all need to remember that message — especially in unfavorable times.

We need to remember — to cling to — that message because you see, as fitting as are the words of St. Paul, so skillfully seized upon by the Reverend Dr. King in his message to a group of aspiring young teachers in the mid 1960s, the message of persistent and relentless perseverance is not limited to those who lead in the classroom; indeed, the words were originally intended for Timothy and his fearful band of Christians in the first century. These words, written as they were from a Roman prison by a traveling preacher who would soon pay for his faith with his life, were to provide encouragement to those for whom the future seemed bleak. In his letter, St. Paul was admonishing Timothy and the others that they should not spread the Good News just when times seemed favorable to do so; they should also spread the Gospel when times seemed hopeless.

When the time seemed right, when the crowd seemed right, when the conditions were just right, they were indeed to teach the Gospel. And when times were harsh, when Evil seemed to be prevailing, when the Good seemed all to die young and the Bad seemed to flourish forever, they were to do the same.

In a pop culture world that instructs us to face any personal or collective tragedy by "seeking closure," our Faith teaches us rather to persevere, to live not pretending the tragedy did not occur, but rather to refuse to allow that tragedy, or any other hardship that we might face, to define the standards by which we will order our lives. If we face plenty or want, ours is to be the same response: to persevere. If we face friend or foe, ours is to be the same response: to persevere. If we are filled with happiness or heartache, ours is to be the same response: to persevere—to convince, to encourage and yes, sometimes even to rebuke — but in all things to persevere.

To persevere is not just to whistle in the darkness, for true perseverance does not ignore the evil; it takes it quite seriously. Rather than cower in the corner, however, the follower of Christ faces evil with the same sort of fortitude that possessed the early saints and martyrs. Jesus never promised that we would be immune from heartache or that we would be safe from sorrow. He promised to give us the strength to endure and He promised us that we would never be alone.

Years ago, as the Advent season of 2001 approached, I had a powerful conversation with a young woman here in Durham. It was the umpteenth installment of a continuing dialogue she and I had shared for almost three years. We'd pondered how those who follow Christ don't get some special suit of armor to protect them from the horrors that seem to abound. We'd often chuckled at the sort of pop theology that essentially says that one should be part of the church because a happy payday — Heaven — is promised to all those who follow Christ. We'd talked about how lonely one can be when surrounded by 2,500 worshipers and yet, how intimidating it can be to seek out a small, well-established congregation within which to sojourn. For these reasons and a host of others, the young woman had been on the periphery of the Church her entire life — close enough to see what was going on, distant enough so as not to be a real part.

At the close of the conversation, she said something quite amazing to me. She said she wanted to be baptized; she'd never received Christ's watermark before. She said she wanted to feel the freshness of the sacred water as it washed over her life, her concerns, her past, and her present.

I said, "That's wonderful. Is it because of September 11?"

"No," she said, "It's in spite of September 11."

She was baptized. Her struggles did not, of course, end that day. I have been strengthened by the courage of our young friend who allowed herself to be caught up within and defined not by horrible tragedy, but rather by the powerful and loving message of Christ, the same Christ who reached out to a young man named Saul as he strode toward Damascus, later to Timothy, still later to Martin Luther King, Jr., and to Ron Hardman. On that day my young friend decided to persevere. Might we all follow in her graceful footsteps as we live out our days.

# 13

# Mary, Mary — Not Contrary

*"How can this be, since I am a virgin?"*

The Gospel appointed for the fourth Sunday of Advent (Revised Common Lectionary — Year B) is the quite familiar "encounter" between the angel, Gabriel, and the young "virgin engaged to a man whose name was Joseph, of the house of David" (Luke 1:27).

With the angel's Annunciation to Mary, Gabriel offers startling news. She is to conceive and bear a son, whom she should name Jesus. This son will be great. He will be called the Son of the Most High. Moreover, Gabriel relates that the Lord will give Mary's son the throne of his ancestor David. That's certainly a lot for a young teenager to digest. The startling news continues:

> He will reign over the house of Jacob forever, and of his kingdom there will be no end." Mary said to the angel, "How can this be, since I am a virgin? (Luke 1:33-34).

Gabriel explained that her son would be conceived through what might be called "Christological parthenogenesis." Instead of utilizing the *usual* biological method to join pairs of chromosomes, the power of the Most High would "overshadow" her and, as a result, Mary's son would be Holy — indeed, he would be called the "Son of God" (Luke 1:35). Mary's response, in the face of such startling, and potentially troubling news: "Here am I, the servant of the Lord; let it be with me according to your word (Luke 1:38).

Over the years, quite a few have refused to take Luke's word, or that of the angel, as to the parthenogenic conception of our Lord. There must be a more "conventional" explanation, some say. One might remember the flood of controversy surrounding the renewed "Search for the Historical Jesus" movement that raged in the public sphere and within parts of the academy (mostly, however, outside the seminary) during the years I was at Duke Divinity School (1986-1989). One particularly popular/unpopular book of that period, *The Illegitimacy of Jesus: A Feminist Theological Interpretation of the Infancy Narratives* (Sheffield Phoenix Press Ltd, 1987; ISBN: 978-1905048847), by the late Jane Schaberg, Professor of Religious Studies and Women's Studies at the University of Detroit - Mercy, from 1977 through 2009, took a particularly provocative stance.

Schaberg, who died in 2012, argued that the Gospel writers, Matthew and Luke, were aware that Jesus had been conceived out of wedlock, probably as a result of a rape of Mary by a Roman soldier. According to Schaberg, the Gospel writers had even left some hints of their knowledge within the Gospels themselves — can you say, *Da Vinci Code?* — but that their main purpose was to *explore* the theological significance of Jesus' birth [my emphasis]. In other words, by relating to the early church that the Anointed One was born in a stable, via the exploitation of a poor, unwed peasant girl named Mary, God *demonstrated* the vindication of the oppressed in a truly miraculous manner.

The reaction to Schaberg's book was predictable. Some praised it as fresh and empowering for women; many others scorned both the book and its author. One person with particularly strong views set fire to Schaberg's car.

Whether you believe Schaberg or St. Luke — I'll choose the latter — one is left, in either case, with the utter scandal of Christ's conception and birth. In first century Palestine, unmarried girls just didn't get pregnant; it wasn't done. As a member of an active Jewish synagogue in Nazareth, Mary would have endured months of scorn and ridicule. Then, when she's at full term, possibly suffering from edema and other discomfort, Joseph tells her they have to travel over to Bethlehem, "for tax reasons." One can almost hear her say, "Oy vey!"

Hundreds of years of Christmas carols have caused us to lose sight of the scandal surrounding the sacred birth. I'm reminded of a conversation I had some years ago with a friend and minister within the United Methodist Church. As we discussed the annual pageantry of Christmas in many small American congregations, my friend — known for his biting sense of humor — quipped, "Isn't it funny that the same sort of parents that would be most scandalized by a grandson born out of wedlock are the very ones to fight to make sure that their 'little Sally' will be cast as Mary in the church Christmas play?"

While most parents would prefer their daughters and sons be married before they conceive, it is, of course, quite common within our culture for children to be born out of wedlock. Each year, approximately one million children are born to fatherless families in America (see, e.g., https://yaleglobal.yale.edu/content/out-wedlock-births-rise-worldwide, last accessed 4/23/2018). That's more than four out of ten (among some American ethnicities, the figure is as high as seven out of ten).

In spite of the relative acceptance of unwed mothers in the secular world around us, they may still feel unwelcome within the church. Recently, I heard a poignant story about a young — and by "young", I mean "early 30s" — *married* woman in the Charlotte area, who happily became pregnant after six years of "trying." Very active in her local congregation, she told many of her friends that she felt as joyous as Elizabeth.

As her months of anticipation passed, her joy was tempered somewhat by discomfort. She began to retain fluids. Alas, there was the day that she had to stop wearing her engagement ring and wedding band; they simply were too uncomfortable. A month or so later, when she was now quite visibly pregnant, she attended a regional meeting of church women within her denomination. At a reception following the primary program, she crossed the fellowship hall to greet a number of women who were from other churches, women whom she had never met.

As she engaged the group in conversation, she quickly saw the face of one of the women light up as the lady said, "Oh, how wonderful! You're expecting." She also saw a look of judgment on the face of another in the group, as that woman first looked at the fullness of the young woman's womb, dropped her gaze to the expectant mother's left hand and, noticing the absence of a wedding band, lifted and turned her head as she abruptly walked away. Would that the church could always greet pregnant women — married or not — in the manner of Elizabeth as she gazed upon her cousin, Mary. "Blessed are you among women ... (Luke 1:42b).

The Protestant church often doesn't know just what to do with Mary. Is she to be lauded because she is somehow the ideal mother? Is she really the *Theotokos* — the God-bearer — as our Orthodox friends believe? Since her death is not recorded in Scripture, was she "assumed" into Heaven without dying, as many within the Roman Catholic and Orthodox traditions believe?

Is she to be scorned because, as some feminists argue, she was too docile, too compliant? Is she to be praised because, as other feminists argue, she was a rebel; read her Magnificat (Luke 1:46, *et seq.*) carefully and you see her boldness. Some — not many — see her as a precursor to the ultimate modern woman: able to have a child without "benefit" of a man.

Last December, I enjoyed an Advent conversation with a close friend who is Roman Catholic. We were discussing the relative roles of Mary of Nazareth within the Roman Catholic and Protestant faiths. He allowed that even in the relatively "low" church group that we know as Methodists, one often sees a church named for St. Mark, St. Stephen, or St. Luke. He added, "I've never seen a St. Mary's UMC."

I nodded, "Nor have I."

There really is a point between the extremes — between venerating Mary to the point of deification (which, contrary to the position of some Protestants, the Roman Catholic Church does **not** do), on the one hand, and ignoring her, on the other. In a true sense, particularly as depicted in Luke's Gospel, Mary may be *the* model for Christian discipleship. She does what is so difficult for most of us. She subsumes her own will within that of Yahweh.

New Testament scholars point out that Luke uses the same verb form to describe the reaction of Zechariah — the father of John the Baptizer — to the news that Elizabeth has conceived as the Gospel writer does to describe Mary's reaction to the "news" from Gabriel. They were both "perplexed" (Luke 1:12, 1:29). Zechariah wants proof, essentially saying he doesn't believe the angel. This angers

Gabriel, who renders Zechariah speechless "until the day these things occur" (Luke 1:20).

Mary, of course, has a question of her own. But hers isn't a statement of disbelief; It's a practical question, "How will this happen?" She's never "known" a man (Luke 1:34). With Gabriel's explanation as to the "how," she is satisfied that she should move forward.

Consider the similarity between Mary's words to Gabriel (Luke 1: 38b) and those of her son later in the Garden, on the night before his death (Luke 22:42). Confronted with the startling news that she will bear a Son, in spite of the fact that she's unmarried, without significant resources, and lives in a world that will surely scorn her, Mary's response is, "Let it be with me according to your word." Sounds a lot like those of her son 33 years later, "Yet, not my will but yours be done." When God breaks into our world—as is God's nature to do—we have two choices. We can believe it or not. Would that our response could echo that of Mary.

# 14

# The Fish that Got Sick to its Stomach

**"Is it right for you to be angry about the bush?"**

I think one reason my childhood was so steeped in Old Testament stories is that many of those "OT" stories are so colorful and susceptible to reenacting within children's Bible School pageants. While six full decades have passed since my early years at Olney Presbyterian, in southern Gaston County (N.C.), the stories (and the pageants) still linger within me. While our teachers always carefully managed to make sure that the stories conformed to a strict "G" rating — that meant skipping "David and Bathsheba," and several others — we nonetheless acted out the tales of Sampson and Delilah, David and Saul, the Tower of Babel, the crossing of the Red Sea, and Noah and the Ark, to mention just a few. One of our favorites was Jonah and the "Great Fish." We mostly followed the King James Version of the Bible, which refers to the sea creature as "a great fish." Newer translations, of course, tend to use "large," instead of "great."

We always stopped our Jonah pageants just after the end of chapter 2, as if the deliverance of Jonah from the gullet of the fish was the climax of the story. It wasn't, of course. There's also the strange, concluding episode involving the sun, the bush, and the worm — an episode that was apparently too theologically challenging for my Olney teachers. It may have been for yours as well.

In the familiar first act, the Lord tells Jonah to go "at once" to Nineveh, a great city, and to cry out against it, since its wickedness offended the Lord. Nineveh, it may be recalled, was the capital city of the Assyrians (i.e., a people who were not part of the twelve tribes of Israel). The place was worse than South Chicago. Nineveh's rulers boasted about how many people they had killed (*see* Nahum 3).

Jonah, it seems, was not an evangelical. The thought of mixing with the teeming mass of sinners inside the wicked city made him nauseous. He headed in the other direction to Joppa, so as to take a ship for Tarshish. Alas, the Lord hurled a great wind upon the sea, the ship was threatened, and even the experienced sailors were frightened, each crying out to "his god" (Jonah 1:5).

In spite of the commotion, Jonah is fast asleep in the hold of the ship. The sailors throw the cargo overboard, as if to appease the gods of the sea. It doesn't work. Sure among themselves that there must be some sort of causal connection between someone on board and the ravaging wind and sea, they cast lots to determine who is at fault and, of course, the lot falls on Jonah. Asked if he has done something to offend "his god," Jonah mutters, "Well, there might be that thing with the Ninevites" (Jonah 1:10).

Thinking that if Jonah's God was powerful enough to send the wind and waves, He might not be pleased if the sailors heaved the Lord's prophet overboard, the sailors sit down and try to row themselves out of their trouble, but to no avail, of course. The crescendo builds until eventually, of course, the sailors give in and throw Jonah into the sea. Immediately there is calm.

Well, not total calm, of course. But we know the rest of Act I pretty well: the great fish swallows Jonah, begins to feel nauseated and, after three days, throws Jonah up on "dry land." Jonah, no doubt by now suffering from PTSD, is instructed a second time to get himself over to Nineveh. This time Jonah obeys, telling the folks over in the capital city that they have 40 days to repent, or else. And a miracle occurs: the people of Nineveh believe God, proclaim a fast, and "everyone, great and small, put on sackcloth" (Jonah 3:5). They thought among themselves, "Perhaps God may relent and change his mind?" God does change God's own mind. God will not destroy Nineveh.

The curtain goes down and everyone lives happily ever after, right? Well, not exactly. Remember: this is the Old Testament. While the Bible School pageant always ended at this point in the story, in the original version, there is still another act to unfold.

Jonah is angry with the Lord. In prayer, he confesses that the reason he initially refused to go to Nineveh was not so much the physical dangers there; he had not feared he might be mistreated, or even killed. Rather, he had refused on theological grounds. He knew what kind of God his Lord was—the kind of God who was "gracious and merciful, slow to anger, and abounding in steadfast love, and ready to relent from punishing" (Jonah 4:1-2). You see, Jonah didn't want to see forgiveness; he wanted to see those in Nineveh suffer and perish. If the Lord wanted to save them, Jonah would just as soon sit down and die.

The Lord then turns to Jonah and asks, "Is it right for you to be angry?" (Jonah 4:4). Jonah ignores the question, treating is as rhetorical, and sits down to see what will happen to the Ninevites.

Of course, Nineveh is adjacent to the desert, where it gets hot. Act II continues with the Lord "appointing" a bush to provide shade from the sun. This made Jonah happy. But then the Lord did an unusual thing: he "appointed" a worm to attack the bush, so that it withered. After the bush had withered, the Lord prepared a dry east wind, and the sun beat down on Jonah until he fainted from the heat. Jonah repeated his earlier entreaty, "It is better for me to die than to live" (Jonah 4:9b).

As Act II closes, the Lord repeats his "rhetorical" question in a slightly different manner, "Is it right for you to be angry about the bush? (Jonah 4:9). Defiant to the end, Jonah responds, "Yes, angry enough to die" (*Id.*).

The final curtain falls as God pricks Jonah's calloused heart with a point that will later be echoed by a wandering, homeless, young rabbi in the early part of the first century:

> You are concerned about the bush, for which you did not labor and which you did not grow; it came into being in a night and perished in a night. And should I not be concerned about Nineveh, that great city, in which there are more than a hundred and twenty thousand persons who do not know their right hand from their left, and also many animals? (Jonah 4:10-11).

Note the similarity between God's questions in Act II of Jonah's story and at least two of the Parables of Jesus — (a) the Parable of the Workers in the Field (Matthew 20:1-16) and (b) the Parable of the Prodigal Son (Luke 15:11-32). In the Matthew parable, the Lord says to the disgruntled workers, "Do you begrudge my generosity?" (Matthew 20:15b). The father of the Prodigal Son, who has thrown the party for the returning sinner asks essentially the same question of the angry, disgruntled and unforgiving son (Luke 15:32).

Eight hundred years after the time of Jonah, the risen Lord forcefully encountered a young Pharisee named Saul, soon to be known as "Paul," as Saul traveled to Damascus to persecute those within the early Church. Saul was told to take the Gospel of Jesus Christ to the people beyond Palestine, most of whom were Gentiles. In this New Testament encounter, the Lord didn't appoint a fish, or a bush, or even a worm. Perhaps mindful of "Act II" of the Jonah story, Paul's response was, "Let's roll."

There's still a broad and expansive world out there, my friends. What say you? Shouldn't we rent a bus and drive to Nineveh? Or are you obsessing over the azaleas?

# 15

# Centering Prayer

"And yet, when the Son of Man comes, will he find faith on earth?"

In some Christian traditions, the Octave Day of Easter (*i.e.*, the Sunday *after* Easter) is called "Low Sunday." While the term's origin is not completely clear, it is generally intended to denote the natural contrast between it and the preceding "High" Easter Sunday. Some Protestant ministers joke that there are actually two "Low Sundays" each year: the Sunday after Easter, to be sure, but also the Sunday after Christmas. They call them "Low Sundays" not so much because of the contrast in the level of worship pageantry, but because the typical attendance in church that day is "low." Attending church on "Low Sunday" — knowing that you are part of the "righteous remnant" — it can generate thoughts of self-satisfaction.

I think that it was that sort of thought process that Jesus had in mind when he told the parable of the Pharisee and the tax collector (Luke 18:9-14). Two citizens go into the Temple to pray. One is a Pharisee; the other is a tax collector. In as much as the

Pharisees maintained their "purity" by separating themselves from others, so here this Pharisee stands by himself to pray. The Pharisee's contempt for others can be seen in his words. While his prayer is one of thanksgiving, his gratitude is that he is not like "other people," particularly "this tax collector" (Luke 18:11).

The Pharisee continues his prayer by reminding God of the Pharisee's religious accomplishments: fasting and tithing are among the many proofs of his piety. The Pharisee asks nothing of God. He is, after all, not a sinner.

In His parable, Jesus contrasts the Pharisee with a tax collector, who also stands alone. Yet the tax collector's "alone" is different; it is "far off" (Luke 18:13a). He is isolated by shame. The tax collector cannot bring himself to assume the usual "stance" for prayer in the time of Christ. Instead of looking up to God, with hands and arms outstretched upward, as was the custom of the time, the tax collector's guilt causes him to bow his head (Christian prayer practices reflect the influence of this parable). Struck with grief, the tax collector can only ask for God's mercy.

The parable, of course, teaches us that the tax collector receives that very mercy. After prayers, he — not the Pharisee — went down to his home "justified" (Luke 18:14). And yet, as my friend, Dr. Richard Lischer, has said on multiple occasions, "In a real sense, *both* men go home justified — one is justified by himself, the other by God."

The parable comes on the heels of a question offered by Jesus, "When the Son of Man comes, will he find faith on earth?" (Luke 18:8). Often, particularly within the Protestant church, that question is rephrased to something like, "Put yourself in the parable. Are you like the Pharisee *or* you like the tax collector?"

Can't you see that for most of us, the answer is, "Yes." We come to worship for many reasons. For some of us, it's simply a matter of habit. For others, it may be "to avoid a fuss." Sometimes we arrive so as to remind ourselves as to how "good" we've been. After all, we serve on this board or that. We're part of an inmate re-entry team. We want to drop off our canned vegetables and macaroni for the homeless shelter's cupboard. We come to offer our regular — no doubt generous — gifts to our church. We're part of the blessed, "Thank you Lord that we are Americans and not Syrians," or, "Thank you Holy One that we don't have three children by three different fathers!" And we go away justified.

Sometimes we come to church to feel small. We come with only a sense of loss and/or brokenness. Our world, or our circumstances within that world, can crush us down so completely that all we can utter is a fervent cry, "Oh, God, be merciful."

Many of us begin our hearing of the parable without recognizing our own tendency to play the role of the Pharisee. We assume that Jesus is talking about others—especially "the Pharisees" that exist in our own world. Yet, by the end of the parable, we may have to confront the Pharisee within our own heart. "**All** who exalt themselves will be humbled, but *all* who humble themselves will be exalted" (Luke 18:14b).

# 16

# Seeing as God Sees

"Are all your sons here?"

Old Testament Scripture teaches us that the last of the so-called "Judges" of Israel was Samuel (see 1 Sam). Based upon Samuel's faithful response to the LORD, wonderful things happened, and the nation of Israel prospered. Under Samuel's faithful leadership, the Israelite army soundly defeated the Philistines, setting into place a long period of peace and prosperity. And everyone lived happily ever after …. Well, not really.

It seems the more you have, the more you have to lose. Not content with Samuel's choice of his own sons as successors, and worried about military and economic threats from their neighbors, the Israelites wanted a king. You know how it often works: your neighbor gets a new deck on the back of his house, you suddenly *need* a new deck. The neighbor installs landscape lights; suddenly you *need* landscape lights. All the neighbors of the Israelites had kings; the Israelites needed a king to feel secure; or at least, they *wanted* one. To the Israelites, apparently the LORD was not enough.

And so, Samuel, with a blessing — and a warning — from the LORD, chose Saul to be Israel's first king. From a physical standpoint, Saul was a perfect 10: strong, tall, dark and handsome. As a king, he was about a four. He disobeyed the LORD in several important fashions and the LORD told Samuel that Saul no longer was looked upon with divine favor.

In Chapter 15 of First Samuel, Samuel publicly breaks the news to Saul that Saul has been rejected by the LORD. Moreover, Samuel tells Saul that the LORD will replace him with another king. Chapter 15 ends with a powerful verse: "And the LORD was sorry that he had made Saul king over Israel."

Well, not as sorry as Samuel, since Samuel is tasked by the LORD with the unenviable job of anointing the new man who would be king. Samuel is worried because Saul, the current king, is still quite alive and quite powerful — powerful enough to have Samuel killed for any insubordination. While Samuel doesn't yet know the exact identity of the next king of Israel, the LORD tells Samuel that he's to journey down to Bethlehem, since the new king is one of Jesse's boys (1 Sam 16:1).

Because of the passage of time, we don't tend to see the scandal in what the LORD has told Samuel. We think, "Yeah, Bethlehem, that's a wonderful place to find a king. That's where Jesus is born." Yet, in Samuel's day — approximately 1,000 B.C. — Bethlehem was on the other side of the tracks. Nearby Jerusalem wasn't yet the capital city. It's as if the LORD had told Durham's local chiefs that the new town leader could be found in a run-down house at the corner of East Pettigrew and South Driver Street. Samuel has to be thinking, "LORD, you don't choose a king from Bethlehem! It just isn't done." And yet, as Samuel is beginning to recognize, the LORD has some funny ideas about how to order the LORD's kingdom. The LORD doesn't follow humanity's rules.

# QUESTIONS OF FAITH

The story continues; Samuel obediently journeys down to Bethlehem. The town fathers there cry out, "Now this is all we need (*see* 1 Sam 16:4). Like Samuel, they were afraid of Saul. Samuel assures them that he's there only to offer a sacrifice — which is, of course, a lie. They likely think to themselves, "Samuel didn't need to come all the way down here from Gibeah in order to offer a sacrifice to the LORD. How dumb does Samuel think we are?"

And yet, the ruse works. Jesse and his sons are invited to the sacrifice, where the sons are presented, one by one to Samuel.

> When they came, he looked on Eliab and thought, "Surely the LORD's anointed is now before the LORD." But the LORD said to Samuel, "Do not look on his appearance or on the height of his stature, because I have rejected him; for the LORD does not see as mortals see; they look on the outward appearance, but the LORD looks on the heart" (1 Sam 16:6-7).

Seven sons walk by and none make the cut. Samuel inquires, "Are all your sons here?" It is only when the youngest son is called in from the fields that we learn who is to be the next king. "Little" David — the smallest son of an unknown member of the smallest clan of the smallest tribe in all of Israel is the one to be anointed with the special oil brought by Samuel: "The last shall be first." Jesse thinks his youngest is so insignificant that Jesse hasn't even bothered to invite him to the party. We see that the LORD has a way of broadening the guest list when it suits the LORD's purposes.

Throughout the history of humankind, it seems the LORD has looked for emissaries of Grace in persons whom society says are unlikely candidates for the LORD'S favor. For example, when it was time to choose who might be the father and mother of "a great nation," God's chosen people, the LORD chose an old man

85

and a barren woman — Abraham and Sarah. The LORD chose the second-born, Jacob — a momma's boy — over his brother, Esau. Yahweh chose Moses, a murderer with an identity crisis, to lead the children of Israel out of Egypt. Yahweh will later choose a barren older woman to conceive and bear John the Baptist and will chose a young, unmarried girl named Mary to be the *Theotokos* — the bearer of God. The LORD, it seems, delights in doing the impossible.

The LORD makes such unusual choices within whom to communicate God's Grace because, as our 1 Samuel text teaches us, "The LORD does not see as mortals see." It's as if we suffer from a type of perverse near-sightedness. We look primarily at the outward appearance, but the LORD looks at the heart. I often wish that I could see others as God sees them.

In March 2017, our youngest grandchild, Everett — son of Blair and Sarah — was baptized at Trinity Avenue Presbyterian Church, where Jane and I regularly worship, during the 11:00 o'clock worship service. It was a special day within the Robinson clan. Not only would Everett receive the special watermark of the Faith, but Pastor Katie had kindly asked me to assist with worship that day in order that I might be part of Everett's baptism. I served as Lector, offered the historic questions of Faith to Blair and Sarah, and I offered the baptismal prayer over the water — big stuff for me.

I had determined to arrive at a few minutes past 10. On my way into town, I decided I'd get one more cup of coffee and a little breakfast, so I pulled into the McDonald's on Miami Boulevard, near the intersection with Highway 70. As I pulled up to the drive-thru line, I noticed three or four cars ahead of me. "Not too bad," I thought. A minute later, still several car lengths from the microphone where I'd place my order, I lowered my window so that I'd be ready to shout my choice to the crew inside.

I was suddenly bombarded by booming music emitted from the car ahead of me. In spite of the fact that there was a real chill to the air — it was March, after all — the driver, a young man in his early 20s, had all four windows down, blasting out the decibels as if there was no tomorrow. I, of course, had been righteously listening to WCPE's "Sacred Music" program; the young man's "noise" now drowning out my Bach. I seethed. "How inconsiderate of that young man to inflict his music tastes upon me? I bet he isn't going to church," I thought to myself.

I determined to engage in a duel of sorts, so I pushed the button to lower my driver's side window all the way and I turned up my sacred melody a bit, although it did nothing to cancel the vibes coming from the car ahead. Both his car and mine seemed to be throbbing to the beat of his music; the vehicles ignoring the lovely melody coming from the small speakers of my little Honda.

I crassly gave my order to the gal on the other side of the microphone and the line of cars inched forward and forward, until it was my turn to handle the transaction at the "pay" window. As you know, you generally pay at the first window and get your food at the second. The young lady inside slid open the window and gave me a cheerful, "Hi!"

I think I probably sneered and rolled my eyes. Pointing to the vehicle in front of me, she quickly said, "See the guy in front of you?"

I said, "Yeah," thinking, of course, that not only had I "seen" him; I had "heard him" now for several minutes and I was not at all pleased.

"Well, he got your breakfast. Have a great day!"

Thomas A. Robinson

The boomerang of my judgment flew back and hit me squarely in the chest. I thought to myself, "the LORD does not see as mortals see." We look at the outward appearance, but the LORD looks at the heart .... I was ashamed of what had been in my heart.

## 17

# Sojourners

"How can this be?"

Eight years ago, I traveled to San Francisco for a Friday morning business meeting, intending to return via a 9:45 a.m. (Pacific time) flight the following morning. Early Saturday, I was startled to hear my cell phone ring in my hotel room at a few minutes past 4:00 a.m.

Jane's voice quickly said, "Tom, everything's OK here, but the airline called to say your flight has been cancelled. They've put you on a later flight that leaves San Francisco at 12:30 this afternoon, but you better check to make sure I heard the details correctly."

I thought, "How can this be?"

A quick e-mail check confirmed my new travel arrangements. I'd be changing planes in Dallas-Fort Worth, instead of Chicago, finally landing at RDU at 11:30 p.m. — two hours later than my original itinerary. I noticed there was only a 40-minute layover in Dallas. Knowing the size of that sprawling airport, my thought was, "Cutting it a bit short."

It hit me that things were potentially problematic when I checked in at the American kiosk at SFO. Instead of a boarding pass, I got a slip that said, "check with an agent."

When I made my way through the snake-like queue, the agent indicated that my "new" departure flight had been "slightly" delayed, that things were going to be tight making the connection in Dallas, but that he thought everything would be ok. He'd seated me as close to the front of the plane as possible; such forward placement would get me to my RDU flight a bit quicker. I indicated that if I missed the last flight to RDU and became stranded in Dallas, someone at the airline would hear about it. Knowing that it wouldn't be him, that if I were stranded in Dallas, it would be a Texas employee who'd be the recipient of my wicked tongue, the agent calmly said, "I think this is going to work."

As I waited in the airport gate area, not quite certain what my options might be, I saw yet another announcement of a further delay. The person at the gate told us anxious travelers that the airline was aware of the tight schedules on some of the connecting flights, that they hoped the pilot would be able to make up some of the time once we departed. Finally, when my mental calculations indicated that if everything worked out just right, I'd still miss my connection, I shuffled down the gangway and took my seat in 12-E (when you get bumped off one flight onto another, you can rest assured that you are in a middle seat).

I put away my carry-on and sat down in my assigned perch, determined to stare a hole through the back of 11-E, the seat in front of me. Within a few minutes, a young man joined me, probably in his mid-twenties. He took the window seat to my right, looking relatively harmless. A minute or two later, a trim woman moved down the aisle and formed the complement to our little trio of airline seats. Clad in an expensive-looking athletic "warm-up" suit — black, trimmed out in white — she quietly put away her travel bag, buckled her seat belt, and opened a sports magazine.

I quickly decided she was one of "those" types that run incessantly, who monitor the fat ratios of their bodies as carefully as CPAs manage corporate ledgers. A small grouping of fine lines around her eyes told me that she was in her early-to-mid forties — about 15 years my junior — certainly well-to-do (what was she doing back here in tourist class), accustomed to spending her summer days at some racquet club in her home town. She'd no doubt met some of her Pinot Noir-sipping girlfriends for a few days shopping in the Bay City. I resumed my efforts visually to bore a hole in the tray table in front of me.

Some few more minutes passed. We had not yet begun our taxi to takeoff. Her voice interrupted my efforts at airline vandalism. "Pardon me," she quietly said, "but you look quite troubled. Something is obviously very wrong. Is there anything I can do to help?"

"No, I'm sorry. Thank you. It's just that I'm going to miss my connection in Dallas. That will mean I don't make it home to North Carolina until tomorrow. The airline cancelled my first flight and should have given me the option of flying on another airline. I'll get to argue with some airline official about what kind of room allowance I'm to be given. It's just really irritating."

"Air travel is really horrible these days," she gently said. "I'm a sales rep for a number of sporting goods lines and I have to be away from home some thirty-five weeks a year. They shuffle you around like cattle, poke and prod you like you're either a drug runner or a terrorist, and act like they're doing you a favor when they pour you four ounces of bottled water, with little or no ice." She added that she was fortunate, that she didn't have to worry about her connection since she was on the continuation flight from Dallas to St. Louis. She couldn't miss her next plane; she was already on it.

I responded that, unlike her, I only had to travel three or four times each year, that I really shouldn't complain, that I was just frustrated, and that I should just hope for the best. She added that from my description of things, the "best" I probably could hope for would be a decent room near the Dallas airport and an early Sunday morning flight back to RDU.

We continued to talk a bit. Seeing her wedding ring, I asked if she had children (always one of my favorite topics and one that normally puts me in a smiling mood). She said yes, that she and her husband had four. She quickly rifled off the names and ages of her brood. Except for her youngest—two years older than our youngest, Gray—her children were exactly the ages of Jane and my offspring (so much for her being 15 years younger than me). Like us, the woman had a daughter and three sons, albeit in a different gender order.

She added, "Don't you just love how much fun they are when they're grown?" I agreed.

Noting our similarities, I said, "I bet you have two grandchildren, an older granddaughter and a younger grandson," thinking hers would surely match our Callie and Jack (Jane and I, of course, have been blessed with four more since this travel encounter).

She retorted, "Well, you're right about the number, but our two are both boys." We continued to laugh at our parallel lives.

We resumed our discussion. Having seen her cross herself as we sped down the runway for take-off, I inquired if she was Catholic. She allowed how the Church was an important part of her life. I shared that I was a sometimes bewildered, well-educated Protestant, but that I'd been to Mass a hundred times. She laughed. We talked on for a good while. She observed how having four children had meant making certain sacrifices. I quickly agreed, thinking and speaking to her about college tuition, and the like.

She smiled and with a twinkle in her eye (or was it a misty, yet happy, tear), added, "God has richly blessed my Daniel and me. Oh, there were certainly times when it was a real struggle. We've both worked pretty hard over these many years, but you know, no one's life is easy. There wasn't always enough money to go around in our house, but there has always been enough love in our hearts."

She paused just a second, "That's God's gift to us; Daniel and I often say. We've learned to give thanks to God at all times for all the blessings that we have."

We continued talking as the flight attendant distributed our refreshments — no free snacks for those of us in the back of the plane. She turned to me, noting the small cups of diet soda on our tray tables, and chuckled, "you get more than this at Mass." I smiled and nodded.

She turned to me and said, "You know, we've followed similar paths over these past many years, but there's one huge difference in our journeys."

I'm sure I had a puzzled look on my face as I said, "Really?"

She responded, "You said you and your Jane have been married thirty-eight years (again, this air travel conversation took place in 2009). Well, as I said, like you, Daniel and I have a 34-year-old." She paused for just a second and continued, "But we've only been married 33 years."

"Ohhhhh," I replied. "That must have been stressful."

"Oh, yes," my friend allowed. "I was only 16 when I found out that I was pregnant. I had our oldest son when I was 17, and my father wouldn't let us get married until I had graduated from high school. So, we were married when I was 18. Daniel is two years older than me."

All I could do was nod.

She paused a bit and pensively looked at some imaginary image in the distance. "Of course, my mother made me go to confession," my new friend said quietly. "Knowing that I had to face the priest made it the longest week of my life. I spent that entire week sketching out suggestions for penance, just in case the priest should ask me what I thought would be appropriate. I wanted so much to be prepared for my encounter with God," she told me. "You know, we Catholics believe that the priest is a proxy for the Lord Himself."

She continued, "I barely got past the 'Bless me Father,' when I burst into tears. I've never cried so unconsolably in my life. I couldn't speak. All I could murmur was 'Father, I'm so, so sorry. Forgive me, please.'"

I, of course, was speechless at this point. The plane's engines droned on behind us. The youngster to my right listened intently to his iPod. The hair on my neck stood up. She continued, her hand now firmly gripping my left arm, just above my wrist.

"As I sat, sobbing in the confessional, the priest leaned toward the screen that separated us and he softly said, 'Mary (notice that until now I haven't told you my new friend's name), I seem to recall a story about another young woman who became pregnant before she was married. My child, things worked out all right.'"

I looked at Mary through a thin sheen of moisture in my eyes and said inadequately, "We all need forgiveness. Thanks be to God."

We talked on for the remainder of the flight, celebrating how each of us had been wonderfully blessed—by caring spouses, wonderful children and grandchildren, steadfast friends and family members, and by a loving God who reaches out to us when we need Him most.

It's so anti-climactic to say that I made my connection, that I waved goodbye to Mary — I never caught her last name — as eight of us ran for the special bus that the airline had waiting on the tarmac, so that we could be carried around to the other side of the huge Dallas-Fort Worth terminal, to catch the last flight to Raleigh-Durham. I arrived at RDU at 11:30 pm, retrieved my car, drove home, and kissed Jane on the forehead as she snuggled in our bed, whispering to her that I had a story to tell her in the morning.

At 7:30 a.m. on Sunday, a good bit later than is my usual custom, I pulled out the Lectionary to see what the readings were for the week. I thought to myself, "Sola Scriptura (my Sunday School Class at Trinity Avenue Presbyterian Church) is going to get a hurried lesson today."

I saw the selected Epistle reading was from Ephesians—Chapter 5. Familiar with the text, I thought to myself, "How can this be?"

> Be careful then how you live, not as unwise people but as wise, making the most of the time, because the days are evil. So do not be foolish, but understand what the will of the Lord is. Do not get drunk with wine, for that is debauchery; but be filed with the Spirit, as you sing psalms and hymns and spiritual songs among yourselves, singing and making melody to God the Father at all times and for everything in the name of our Lord Jesus Christ (Ephesians 5:15-20).

I scanned and confirmed the familiar verses, particularly verse 16: "making the most of the time, because the days are evil," and I remembered that many scholars (including the Rev. Dr. Richard Lischer, who first shared this point with me some years ago) think the better translation of the first part of the verse is that of the old King James Version: "redeeming the time."

I thought back to my mood in San Francisco the previous day, at how angry and thankless I'd been at the beginning of my flight.

I recalled how my mood had changed as I made a new friend, that in our own way, Mary and I had "made melody to the Lord" in our hearts, and I realized that in a deeply profound and spiritual sense, Mary had *redeemed* time.

    Thanks be to God.

# 18

# Death's Defeat!

"Where, O death, is your victory? Where, O death is your sting?"

Some years ago, Jane and I journeyed from Durham down to Charlotte for a party celebrating the upcoming wedding of our youngest, Gray, and his fiancé, April Robertson. The party was the one in a long series of somewhat similar gatherings that took place over a decade and a half among eight couples who have been close friends for more than forty years. With the exception of one Converse College graduate and me, a Demon Deacon/Blue Devil, everyone in the group had been a student at Erskine College — a small church-related liberal arts college in Due West, S.C. — during the late 60s and early 70s. When any of our children have married, the couples within the Erskine enclave have given a party for the young happy couple. As you can imagine, at any of these parties the former Erskine students and the two add-ons — now gray-headed and somewhat slower of foot than when we forged our friendships in Abbeville County, S.C. — have enjoyed ourselves even more than the particular young couple being honored.

This particular evening, as we shared some wonderful lasagna and not a little wine, one of the Erskine guys inquired, "Where are the six jugs hidden?"

"Six jugs?" another friend retorted.

"Sure, if we run out of wine, we can fill the jugs with water and make some more wine," mused the first of my buddies.

> On the third day there was a wedding in Cana of Galilee, and the mother of Jesus was there. Jesus and his disciples had also been invited to the wedding. When the wine gave out, the mother of Jesus said to him, "They have no wine!" Now standing there were six stone water jars for the Jewish rites of purification, each holding twenty or thirty gallons. Jesus said to them, "Fill the jars with water." And they filled them up to the brim. He said to them, "Now draw some out, and take it to the chief steward." So they took it. When the steward tasted the water that had become wine, and did not know where it came from (though the servants who had drawn the water knew), the steward called the bridegroom and said to him, "Everyone serves the good wine first, and then the inferior wine after the guests have become drunk. But you have kept the good wine until now." Jesus did this, the first of his signs, in Cana of Galilee, and revealed his glory; and his disciples believed in him (John 2:1-11).

During the conversations of the evening, as the group shared stories related to our children's' nuptials that have taken place in somewhat disparate locales — Durham, Knoxville, Charleston, Rock Hill, Charlotte, Greenville, S.C., among others — I was reminded of one particular wedding. It had been celebrated a number of years earlier in Darlington, South Carolina, where Henry and Anne Funderburk, one of the Erskine couples, have spent most of the decades since the glorious summer of 1971 — the summer the Funderburks and the Robinsons were married. Anne was Jane's roommate at Erskine. Anne and Henry had no more sense than Jane and me and so both couples married after our sophomore year in college. While there have been some bumps in the road — there always are — both couples have been truly blessed for more than four decades.

That July we traveled to Darlington to be present for the wedding of Amy, the youngest of Anne and Henry's three children. Now, of course, Darlington isn't exactly a destination spot. It's a slow-paced village, with an old-fashioned town square. I-95 comes no closer than five miles; the U.S. Highway 52 By-Pass means you can swing around the town from the other direction without so much as a glance. In most respects (except on NASCAR race day), Darlington's quite ordinary. That makes it a lot like Cana in Galilee.

You know, there's nothing like the hug from an old friend. Nothing stirs your pride like the glimpse of two strong, young men — wasn't it just yesterday that Hal and Michael were mischievous little boys? And there is nothing that is as beautiful as a friend's eyes that at first glisten and then well up with tears as you exchange simple words:

"I'm so glad you could come;"

"Oh, we wouldn't have missed it for the world."

Jane and I didn't get a chance to read the Sunday morning newspaper in Darlington, the day after the wedding. Small town papers still include the sort of small town pieces about garden parties, anniversary gatherings, weddings, and the like. I trust the newspaper mentioned the exquisite music played by the four-piece ensemble during the wedding service. I'll bet it described Amy's gown; she was stunning. The writeup may even have included a comment about the big grin on the young groom's face as he nervously walked to the altar and then looked up and saw the assembled wedding party in the back of the church. I doubt, however, that it mentioned Amy's "going away" dress.

I doubt the writeup mentioned that the dress had actually been purchased more than 50 years ago, that it had been worn by Amy's maternal grandmother in the early 1960's. The dress, of course, was never actually worn by a grandmother; the striking young woman for whom it was first fitted would die without ever seeing either of her daughters — much less a grand-daughter — walk down the wedding aisle. That slender young woman would never enjoy the tenderness of holding the child of her own child, would never be the giver of matronly advice, would never be able to dote upon a little one as only a grandmother can do.

I doubt the writeup mentioned that the dress was one of only a few keepsakes that our friend, Anne, has, that she and Henry lost virtually all their family treasures and memorabilia in a fire some years before Amy's wedding. In the fire, they lost not just furniture and fixtures; they lost all the children's first shoes and toys, the photographs, the report cards and third grade projects — all those worthless, yet priceless, trinkets that help parents mark the passage of the years. Somehow the dress, Anne's mother's dress, had been safely stored elsewhere.

In late Spring of young Amy's wedding year, as Anne and Amy were making final plans for July19th, as Henry was no doubt worrying what the final tally would be, there was an important item not checked off their to-do list: the "going away" dress. Nothing Amy tried seemed to work. The style of this one was ok, but the color was really wrong. Another looked great, but my, what a sticker price. A well-intentioned friend had seen a possibility in a nearby shop — no, it would never do. At wit's end, mother turned to daughter and said, "you know, there's one more dress you should see."

Like water turned to wine, as soon as the heirloom touched Amy's skin, it was transformed from tailored cloth to vestal garment. Needing no alterations whatsoever, the dress adorned the bride-to-be as if it had been handsewn specifically for her. There was never a question in their minds. Both Amy and her mother knew they'd found the dress, or rather, the dress had found them. Aided, I'm confident, by the power and presence of the resurrected Lord who joyfully graces His flock at a wedding, a young woman's love had reached across decades of time, across space, across the face of Death itself, to present a gift to the grand-daughter the woman had never met. "Where, O death, is your victory? Where, O death is your sting?" [1 Cor 15:55].

And so, it was that after the wedding that warm July evening, after several hours of dancing and fun at the wedding reception, Amy quietly excused herself and, with her mother's help, changed from her wedding gown into her grandmother's dress. At a few minutes past 11:00 pm, Amy stepped from the dressing room into the sometimes scary, always exciting, and yet uncertain world of adulthood and marriage. She did so confidently, clothed as she was in the special dress provided by her young grandmother, surrounded as well by the unconditional love of her parents, and the devoted commitment of her young husband.

For those of us who knew the story of the dress, it was a powerful moment. To see three generations joined so incredibly — it takes my breath even now to think about it. On one level, I am struck with the poignant knowledge that as He had done at Cana, Christ was at it again, gracing a wedding as he had done twice in August 1971. At yet another level, I realize that Cana is also an Epiphany story that the resurrected Christ's presence promises not only abundance, but victory. Death does not have the last word. Christ does.

"Where, O death, is your victory? Where, O death is your sting?"

Oh, by the way, a few years after her wedding day, Amy gave birth to a daughter of her own. "Praise God from Whom All Blessings Flow."

# 19

# Knitting Lessons

"Do we know if they were girls or boys?"

As I have mentioned, both within and without these pages, God's Kingdom is such an inversion of the world around us that things often get turned upside-down. Teacher becomes student — a father or mother is taught by the child. I recall one such instance that occurred 30 years ago, when our son, Blair, was about seven years old. These days, of course, Blair experiences similar "inversions" of his own, as he sits at the feet of his and Sarah's daughter, Emory, and son, Everett (the latter is still too young to be an effective teacher).

This, like so many other inversion lessons, came to me because I was not anticipating anything significant. It was a clear, beautiful Spring day and I had apparently dropped Anna and Walker somewhere; only Blair was in the back seat of the car (son, Gray, only two years old, was likely at home with Jane). As I drove, I listened to the radio, maneuvered the car through the streets of Durham, and mentally went down my list of to-do items, attempting to determine how they might be balanced in the upcoming days. A voice from the back seat interrupted my rumination, "Daddy, so Mama had two babies who died before they were born?"

"What?" I thought. "What?" I said.

"Mama — did she have two babies in her belly that died before they were born?"

"Err, yes — not at the same time, of course — but yes, yes, she did. Why would you ask?"

Indeed, Jane had suffered two miscarriages, one early-on, at about eight or ten weeks, between the births of Anna and Walker, the other when she was much further along. That second miscarriage occurred some three years after Blair's own birth. We had shared this information with Anna and Walker. I'm not sure we had done so at that point in Blair's life, but intimate family sorrows quickly spread from child to child, as you know.

Blair did not respond to my question. I settled back into my driving/planning mode, sure that the issue had passed. Fully three or four minutes later, I heard another question from behind my head, "Daddy, do we know if they were girls or boys?"

"Uh, uh, we're not certain about the first, but we think they were both boys," was my stuttered reply.

> For it was you who formed my inward parts, you knit me together in my mother's womb" (Ps 139:13).

Several more minutes passed without any further response from Blair. Then suddenly the lesson came, uttered as it was from child to parent, "So I've got two brothers in Heaven who I've never met."

I almost drove off the road, as I inadequately responded, "Yes, Blair, I suppose you do." The thoughts rolled over and over in my head. After some additional time had passed — it may have been a few seconds, it may have been much, much longer — I thought to myself, "And I have two sons that I haven't met ... yet."

Blair, it seemed, had captured the core idea of the Psalmist. God's relationship with us is so strong, so intimate, so powerful, that it begins long before we ever draw breath. It's a bond that, through the love and sacrifice of Christ, is also unbreakable and never-ending. Thanks be to God!

# 20

# The Issue of Abortion — How Things "Really Are"

"In the resurrection, therefore, whose wife will the woman be?"

A consistent characteristic of the Christian perspective is the extent to which it has often stood in opposition to opinions and beliefs pervasive within society. This was as true in Jesus' time as it is today. One such example from the time of Christ can be seen in chapter 20 of the Gospel according to St. Luke. The Sadducees (who say there is no resurrection) pose a hypothetical question to Jesus concerning a woman who is married to seven brothers successively, each of whom dies without producing any children. In the resurrection, as described by Jesus, "which brother's wife will she be? All seven have married her" (Luke 20: 33).

It was certainly a legitimate question, for the standards of that society dictated that a woman was to be defined primarily in terms of to whom she was married, not on a more personal basis. That the woman would have to be married to one of the men, even in the so-called resurrection — if there was one — seemed obvious to the Sadducees. Their hypothetical question dealt with life as they saw it. Jesus' response that in the age to come she would be married to no one, that instead she would be like an angel—indeed, a daughter of God—was in stark opposition to conventional thought of that day. As Dr. Tom Long (Bandy Professor of Preaching at Candler School of Theology, Emory University, in a sermon preached years ago at Duke Chapel, Durham, North Carolina) has so aptly exhorted, the Sadducees were accurate in describing how things were, but Jesus added an extra and unforeseen dimension to the conversation by describing how things *really* were.

Concurrent with the march of technology, the progression of medical techniques, and the increase in scientific knowledge, we are faced today with tough questions, many of which are not hypothetical. They tax our ability to formulate appropriate responses. Few questions, if any, seem as tough as those concerning abortion. Abortion is a fact of life, or rather a fact of death. Substantial debate continues, but it is relatively clear which acts are prohibited and which others prescribed within the secular American society.

Abortion is a popular method of birth control in America. While the number has dropped in recent years from the highs we experienced in the 1990s, when I published an earlier version of this piece (*See* "The Issue of Abortion: How Things "Really Are," *Encounter: Creative Theological Scholarship*, Autumn 1995, vol. 56, no. 4, pp. 335-341), more than 900,000 abortions took place in 2015 — the last year for which relatively complete data is available (note that while the Centers for Disease Control reports fewer abortions each year, a number of states, including California — our most populous — Maryland, and New Hampshire, do not report their respective numbers to the CDC). Indeed, almost 17 percent of all American pregnancies are terminated by an abortion. In New York City, one in four pregnancies are deliberately terminated. Since 1973, nearly 53 million legal abortions have been performed in the United States. Indeed, abortion has received the sanction of the sovereign state.

We have a host of secular, civil authorities from which we can draw a picture as to "how things are" within the womb. In *Eisenstadt v. Baird*, 405 U.S. 438 (1972), the U.S. Supreme Court indicated the constitutional right to privacy meant the *individual* — note the argument regarding "individuality" below — is to be free from unwarranted governmental intrusion into such matters as the issue of whether to bear or beget a child.

*Roe v. Wade*, 410 U.S. 113 (1973), tells us that during the first trimester of gestation, it is really none of *our* business that a woman might decide to abort her fetus and that it is a concern to us during the second trimester only to the extent that the states may reasonably regulate the standards of safety to be employed for the procedures.

*Planned Parenthood of Southeastern Pennsylvania v. Casey*, 505 U.S. 833 (1992), concludes that while a state may discourage or delay an abortion, while it may force a woman to examine evidence or review arguments against abortion, it may not prohibit the abortion, if the fetus has reached the point of viability.

I, of course, use the word "fetus" advisedly. What one calls the mass growing within the womb of the pregnant woman is often an indication of the direction one takes within the abortion discussion. For those who might want to argue in favor of the autonomy of the woman, a great deal is at stake in using terms such as "undifferentiated human tissue" or "blastocyst." Better yet, they often choose not to refer to the fetus at all, but rather to concentrate on and describe the process — "the pregnancy." After all, they see the abortion as merely ending the pregnancy, not a life. For those who support a ban — or near ban — on abortion, great care is given to describing the fetus as "child," "being," or "person."

Notwithstanding the legality and availability of abortions, the so-called "pro-life" proponents have not given up their fight. The debate postulated by the anti-abortionists is no "silent scream." It is robust and loud, threatening those who disagree with potent means such as a national constitutional convention, economic boycott, and civil (as well as "uncivil") disobedience. The opponents of abortion have offered alternative means of describing "how things are" within the womb. Generally, they have concentrated their arguments on the beginning moments of human life, arguing that life begins at conception, as if by proving that thesis, by winning that battle, the rest of the world would follow.

Today there is a compelling need for Christians to examine these real issues and formulate a witness to the world, both without and within the Church. We need, however, not to join the groups attempting to describe matters as they are, but instead, to witness to the way things *really* are.

How then have the secular, civil authorities (joined, unfortunately, by most mainline Protestant denominations) missed the mark? At least in part, they err in as much as they have traditionally placed great and undue emphasis on the doctrine of "viability."

> With respect to the State's important and legitimate interest in potential life, the "compelling" point is at viability. This is so because the fetus then presumably has the capability of meaningful life outside the mother's womb. State regulation protective of fetal life after viability thus has both logical and biological justifications. If the State is interested in protecting fetal life after viability, it may go so far as to proscribe abortion

during that period, except when it is necessary to preserve the life or health of the mother (*Rowe v. Wade*, 410 U.S. at 163).

While the idea of the isolated infant, functioning on his or her own, without need or benefit of mother's protective cavity and life-support, is consistent with the popular idea of individuality and personal freedom within much of America and the western world, it is inconsistent with the proclamations of confessing Christians who see ourselves and others as integral parts of the body of Christ, dependent and interdependent. Who, for example, is actually capable of sustained and "meaningful" life on his or her own?

Our Christian witness to society should be that the gestation period cannot neatly be divided into trimesters, with such division being roughly commensurate with movement toward "viability." Our witness should instead be that Life is not to be defined as the mere ability to eat, respire, produce waste — all "on our own." To the extent that viability is described in terms of "autonomous and independent life," our Baptism calls upon us always to remain *nonviable*.

Many "pro-life" opponents of the civil authority have missed the mark in a different way. They have concentrated on the issue of the inception of human life. But is there really any substantial difference of opinion as to when human life begins? There seems to be virtual unanimity according to so-called scientific standards, that the zygote is alive, that the early embryonic stages involve living matter. Each one grows, responds to stimuli, respires, produces waste matter.

Noted bioethicist, Richard McCormick, challenges us to put one hundred biologists and geneticists in a room and ask them the question of when human life begins. His contention is that the resounding answer will be at the point of fertilization (*See* Shannon,

Thomas A., "Abortion: A Changing Morality and Policy," *Bioethics*, New York: The Paulist Press, 1981, p. 27). All medical evidence indicates that the blastocyst is a complete entity, that it may not resemble a gurgling baby girl or boy, but that it is genetically unique (unless, like me, it's an identical twin), and very much distinct from the unfertilized egg or the sperm.

There also seems to be substantial agreement that the tissue is, in fact, human. Dr. Robert Edwards, co-progenitor of the first "test-tube" baby, anthropomorphically referred to that historic human being as a "she," even though "she" consisted of only eight cells (*See* Kass, Leon R., *Toward a More Natural Science*, New York: The Free Press, 1985, p. 104). As Leon Kass indicates, the blastocyst may not be a "person," but it is certainly "human." It is human in origin and potentially a mature human being — if all goes well.

Many anti-abortionists thus seem intent upon waging a battle that is already won. It is as if the conferring of personhood on the embryo (blastocyst, fetus, etc.) will grant it (be "it" male or female) inviolable rights to life, liberty, and the pursuit of happiness. The fact of the matter is that our society rather routinely makes policy decisions which, if not intentionally resulting in death to human beings, have as a direct and proximate consequence the forfeiture of human life.

We send our boys (and since the first Iraqi War, some of our girls) off to battle with the sure knowledge that some or many of them will not return. We allow the production of alcoholic beverages, cigarettes, and opioids, notwithstanding the sure and total knowledge that the use of such substances will result in the death of many persons each year. We proscribe certain negative behavior, such as murder or some rapes, and execute some of those who violate the statutory code because such actions are deemed particularly malevolent. It seems that life outside the womb is not always sheltered, nor perhaps should it be. Should we expect life within the womb to be absolutely and totally different? No, if we are to protect the "life" of the blastocyst (embryo, fetus, child), we must do more than merely label it "human."

Both sides to the controversy have become caught up within an adversative argument over rights. Each side's description of the facts of life and death seem complete and accurate from the standpoint of the proponents. There is no reason to believe that persons outside the Body of Christ, outside the gathered community of believers, would respond in any other fashion than a recital of individualistic rights. Those of us who feel *our* rights expand and extend to the point at which they touch the nose of our neighbor will always have difficulty understanding our own rights vis-a-vis a neighbor who can accurately be described only as a small mass or number of largely undifferentiated cells with no cerebral cortex, no central nervous system — indeed, no nose. Nor can we hope for different dialogue from a group of professing Christians who appear to be more comfortable walking the picket than they are the *Via Dolorosa*.

Rather than becoming caught up within the individualistic arguments of the secular world or giving our Christian proxies to the so-called "pro-lifers," we, the gathered community, the Body of Christ, should be busy reminding ourselves and those around us that the issues are not resolved by debating which of several groups has the dominant right. Such an activity quickly digresses into the underlying issue of *who* we are. We should instead become involved within the issue of *whose* we are.

Concentrating on *who* we are inevitably places us in an adversative position with others when our Master impels us to avoid the very locus. It allows us, the "un-pregnant," to search diligently for the splinter in the eye of the unwed mother and/or father and fail to see the log in our own. It allows us magnanimously to declare that we are "surrogate" parents of the unborn, but apparently not of the unborn's parents. It allows us, the righteous, simultaneously to waive an American flag and carry the placard "Abortion Kills Children," while we forget or ignore the fact that War Kills God's Children of All Ages.

Concentrating on *who* we are allows us, the "pregnant" to hold onto the prevalent modern notion that what we do with "our bodies" or with our own lives is a matter of concern only to us. It allows us, the careless, to rationalize that we are, after all, only talking about issues of reproductive freedom, rather than issues of sin. It allows for a certain class of "victims," such as the raped, but provides no escape for many others for whom a pregnancy and birth will be equally devastating.

Concentrating on *who* we are allows us to label some of God's creation as wanted and others unwanted. It allows us to brand some unborn children as "problems," as if we are fit and able to make such characterizations. It allows us to decide that one portion of the Body of Christ, to-wit; the womb, the fetus, the marriage, the individual *cum* career, is more important than another when we have come to believe that each part is absolutely indispensable to the whole. It allows us to await an abortion decision from the United States Supreme Court, as if that secular body could give a pronouncement about a matter that is central to our faith. Concern about *who* we are inevitably leads to simple answers to complex questions, a description of the way things are, but rarely a description of the way things *really* are.

And how are things, really? Or, in other words, in the time of the resurrection, to whom will the child about which we speak belong? This is the significant question and it is *not* a rhetorical one.

As with you and me, and with her mother, the child will be like an angel, a son or daughter of God.

## Postscript: Mainline Protestant Church's "Problem" With Abortion

> "And why has this happened to me, that the mother of my Lord comes to me? For as soon as I heard the sound of your greeting, the child in my womb leaped for joy" (Luke 1: 43-44).

Twenty-two years ago, when I wrote the foregoing piece on abortion, I posited that the "Christian perspective" often stands in opposition to opinions and beliefs that are pervasive within society. The Christian perspective is, of course, far from monolithic. Some parts of the Church—the Roman Catholic and Eastern Orthodox Churches, together with many so-called "Evangelical" parts of the Body of Christ — oppose abortion under virtually all circumstances.

Would that mainline Protestantism offered a clear statement as to how things "really are" when it comes to abortion. Unfortunately, virtually all mainline Protestant denominations have thrown in the towel and given their proxies to the so-called pro-choice movement.

For example, the United Methodist Church ("UMC") says that its belief in the sanctity of unborn human life makes it "reluctant to approve abortion" (*The Social Principles*, United Methodist Church). While affirming the sanctity of *unborn* human life, the UMC appropriately acknowledges that the pregnant woman is *also* a life of sacred worth. Without providing any specific examples, the UMC goes on to say there are "tragic conflicts of life with life that may justify abortion, and in such cases, it supports the legal option of abortion under proper medical procedures by certified medical providers" (*Id.*).

The UMC opposes the use of so-called "late-term" abortion (unless the life of the mother is in danger or in the case of severe fetal anomalies incompatible with life). It also stresses that sex-selective abortion is morally indefensible. That is to say that if the woman doesn't want a daughter — only a son — the UMC says that it is morally reprehensible for the woman to abort. If, instead, the woman doesn't want a child at all; well, then, of course, it's ok.

The UMC observes that while precise estimates vary, there are now tens of millions of "missing women" in the world thanks to sex-selective abortions (see http://www.umc.org/what-we-believe/gender-selective-abortion, last accessed May 25, 2018). The UMC apparently fails to see the irony in its statement. Is there no similar lament for the millions of missing American men (and women) who have been aborted in the U.S. since *Roe v. Wade*?

The only significant difference between the UMC's stance on abortion and that of pro-choice Americans is that the UMC wrings its hands and suggests prayer before the abortion occurs. It advises the woman to search the Scriptures (see http://www.umc.org/what-we-believe/the-united-methodist-church-and-the-complex-topic-of-abortion). The church does not appear, however, to provide any helpful scripture references on any of its web sites.

The UMC allows that the abortion issue is, after all, "complex" (*Id.*). Of course, the UMC takes strong stands on a host of other societal issues: minimum wage, immigration, climate change, and equal pay, to name just a few. Does the UMC suggest these other issues are not complex?

As with the UMC, there is little wiggle room between the stance of the Presbyterian Church (U.S.A.) ("PCUSA") and the pro-choice proponents. The 217th General Assembly of the PCUSA acknowledged the inherent difficulty that "an individual woman" [the PCUSA's words, not mine] faces when deciding "whether to terminate a pregnancy." Notice two points.

First, like many within the secular, "pro-choice" movement, the PCUSA shifts the reference point away from "the unborn" and toward a less animate subject: the "pregnancy" (*See* http://www.presbyterianmission.org/what-we-believe/social-issues/abortion-issues/). After all, we're not terminating a "life" here, certainly not a life created in the image of God — we're merely ending a pregnancy.

Second, there is no mention, of course, to the father. In as much as the PCUSA is in lock-step with the pro-abortion movement, it begins its own discussion of the "difficult" issue by framing the entire dialogue in the language of reproductive rights. In the PCUSA's mind, the father has no role to play within the abortion decision.

Like the UMC, the PCUSA gives lip service to the notion that abortion should not be used as a method of birth control. Like so many others within mainline Protestantism, it's apparently blind to the irony in its statements. If abortion isn't birth control, what is it?

To the extent that the UMC fails to offer up examples wherein a woman might be ethically justified in having an abortion, the PCUSA, in its 1992 Report of the Special Committee on Problem Pregnancies and Abortion, offers up a list of nine:

- Pregnancies that will result in a baby with congenital anomalies, inborn errors of metabolism, or inherited diseases.
- Pregnancies that result from rape and incest. We would include in these categories any sexual activity without consent with strangers, friends, partners, or husbands, and sexual activity with relatives. This category would also include women unable to give informed consent because of

a mental or physical handicap.
- Pregnancies in which the baby is exposed to the potential transmission of HIV, or to a congenital defect induced by self-administered or prescribed drugs, industrial chemicals or toxins, alcohol, x-ray or radioactive exposure, or other probable causes of serious deformity.
- Cases of multiple pregnancy in which reduction to a safe number of fetuses is needed.
- Pregnancies resulting from failed contraception.
- Pregnancies where continuation will threaten the life or emotional well-being of the mother, such as recent breast cancer, terminal stages of cancer, major trauma, severe depression or schizophrenia, or advanced cardiovascular disease.
- Pregnancies in which continuation will cause significant economic problems.
- Pregnancies in which age, either below 15 or over 40, places the woman at increased risk of complications.
- Pregnancies among women who have suffered a disastrous or very stressful previous pregnancy and do not believe they are able to face a subsequent pregnancy.

While some potential "problems" associated with pregnancy listed by the PCUSA are both specific and rare, at least two are so broad as to encompass virtually any unborn: (a) pregnancies that might cause economic hardship and (b) those that result from "failed contraception." As to the latter, the PCUSA offers no definition of "failed contraception." For example, would a last second, "I pray I don't get pregnant" qualify? As to the former, have you checked the difference in the medical expense deductibles between an individual and a family health care plan under the Affordable Care

Act? Alternatively, have you noticed the huge increases recently in college tuition? Raising children is expensive! If parents only had the children they could truly afford, there would be far fewer of us walking around.

Can the PCUSA faithfully take a position that counterbalances life with economic and social concerns? Is life less valuable than money, pride, or convenience? Can an abortion ever truly be justified based upon the right of a woman to control her own body when the unborn, though dependent upon, is not a part of the mother's body? It is rather the body and life of another human being entrusted to her for care and nurture.

Indeed, the PCUSA (and most other mainline Protestant denominations) want to blow both hot and cold. On the one hand, it finds appropriate fault with the so-called modern obsession with individualism, teaching and preaching instead each week that we are all part of the Body of Christ, that we are dependent and interdependent. On the other hand, faced with the *perfect* example of such a dependent-interdependent relationship — that between the unborn and his or her mother — the PCUSA says the bond can be destroyed whenever one side of the equation deems it to be "a problem." Can we also abandon the homeless or poor? After all, missional activity can cause a local congregation "significant economic problems."

It is truly ironic that the very existence of the Church is based upon a "problem pregnancy" (Mary's pregnancy would easily have qualified under one or more of the PCUSA categories). Indeed, since Sarah was old and barren, God's covenant with Abraham regarding the nation of Israel — indeed, all nations — was "problematic" as well. According to the PCUSA categories, both the prophet, Samuel, and John the Baptizer were products of problem pregnancies. And yet, Elizabeth, when she was visited by Mary, saw not a problem, but her Lord. Speaking to the *Theotokos*, Elizabeth cried out in joy, "Blessed are you among women, and blessed is the fruit of your womb. And why has this happened to me, that the mother of my Lord comes to me?" (Luke 1:42-43). All this seems to beg the question: Where would the Jewish and Christian Faiths be *without* problem pregnancies?

And yet, most mainline Protestant denominations seek always and everywhere to protect a woman's right to choose death for her unborn child, rather than to lift up the unborn as a daughter or son of God. We pray weekly for "justice." How can there ever be justice when the "least of these" — the ones who can't speak for themselves, who are given no choice at all — are disposed of as if they are refuse?

We offer prayers of confession concerning how we, both individually and as a collective body, shirk our responsibilities and squander the resources God has so lovingly provided. Then we promulgate church doctrine that casts aside God's greatest gift: humanity itself. We give lip service to a "God of the Impossible" and yet teach and foster doctrines that judge the unborn in much the same way as an accountant might judge the value of a piece of equipment. Alas, we become spiritual paupers in the process.

# 21

# Dead Man Talking: Maundy Thursday and the 11th Commandment

"Lord, where are you going?"

Back in law school, we learned that one of the exceptions to the so-called "hearsay rule" — the rule that generally excludes from the jury's ear any statement made outside the courtroom — relates to statements made by persons who know that their death is imminent. The legal logic, while now considered "quaint" by many, is that such deathbed statements are unusually trustworthy; most people don't want to die with a lie on their lips. According to the law, therefore, we should listen carefully to those who know that they are about to leave this world.

During any Lenten season, as we move toward Maundy Thursday, particularly as we consider the scripture that is appointed for that special day, we ought to be particularly mindful of the words of our Lord. In a literal sense, He's a "dead man talking" since, as the scriptures relate, Jesus understood "that his hour had come to depart from this world and go to the Father" (John 13: 1b).

Judas knows that his own plans are now complete. Peter is confident that he will never deny his Lord. The rest echo that likewise they will not forsake Jesus. The stage is set; the die is cast. The drama that begins with an intimate supper shared among the closest of friends and which continues — at least according to John's version — with the Master's act of washing the feet of His followers, will soon end with an arrest, the scattering of those closest to Jesus, some questioning, torture, a long walk with a cross, and finally, death on a hill that sits adjacent to Jerusalem's garbage dump.

And so, after the supper (and the foot washing), mindful of what lies ahead, Jesus turns to his disciples and says:

> I give you a new commandment, that you love one another. Just as I have loved you, you also should love one another (John 13:34).

The Vulgate Bible — the Fifth Century Latin translation attributed to Saint Jerome — *translates* (recall that Jesus generally spoke Aramaic, not Latin or Greek) the text as follows: "Mandatum novum do vobis ut diligatis invicem sicut dilexi vos."

While the church could have chosen a number of different adjectives to describe the penultimate day of Jesus' life, eventually it chose a derivation of the first Latin word of what we might call the Eleventh Commandment — this *new* commandment: "Mandatum novum." Instead of Treacherous Thursday, or Denial Thursday, we observe *Maundy Thursday*. We acknowledge — and celebrate — our new mandate: that we are to love one another. Our Master has commanded that we do so. And this isn't some "do as I say, not as I do" statement. Jesus provided/provides the example of the type of love that we are to show to others: a forgiving love, an extravagant love, a sacrificial love.

A minister friend of mine says that Christ was pretty simple and straightforward: "He obeyed, He loved, and He died." We are to follow His path. As Dietrich Bonhoeffer so effectively observed, "When Christ calls a man [or a woman], He bids him [her] come and die" (*The Cost of Discipleship*, London: SCM Press, 1948/2001), p. 44).

The Christian faith calls *every one* of us to emulate our Lord. And note that we are not just supposed to love one another; we're supposed to love each other *the way that Christ has loved us*. That means that if we are to be true to the words of the Master, we must also serve, obey, love, and die to ourselves. Moreover, we aren't to do it in order to win a prize. We aren't supposed to love each other so that we may gain the Kingdom. Using "Southern" English, we don't love one another so that we can "go to Heaven." We're supposed to love each other because that's what our Lord commanded that we do. The Eleventh Commandment — it isn't easy, but it's true.

# 22

# The Good Friday Tree

"Why, what evil has he done?"

A number of years ago, during "children's time" of a Lenten worship service at Asbury United Methodist Church, I shared with some youngsters the legend of the dogwood tree. You've no doubt heard it: because then it was tall and strong, the dogwood tree was selected to make the Cross of Jesus. Taking pity upon it, Jesus promised that thereafter it would never again grow into a sufficient specimen to be used for such ugly work. The legend continues that Jesus also caused its blossoms (the state flower of North Carolina) to resemble a cross, with tell-tale stains of blood.

One of the kids in the Asbury circle looked at me and said, "Since it's legend, I guess that means it really isn't true."

But another youngster added, "Well whatever tree they used, I'm sure it didn't like it."

But the chief priests stirred up the crowd to have him release Barabbas for them instead. Pilate spoke to them again, "Then what do you wish me to do with the man you call the King of the Jews?" They shouted back, "Crucify him!" Pilate asked them, "Why, what evil has he done?"

After my encounter with the children noted above, the Crucifixion, from the viewpoint of "the Tree," haunted me for a number of years, finally prompting me to write the following poem:

### The Good Friday Tree[2]

Have you not pitied the poor wood
Upon whose frame they lay His tired body to be killed?
Have you wondered how that old tree must have desired
To scream a sense of its own agony as the nails were pounded
First into His flesh and then into its own?

Would that it had been the fig tree which had yielded no fruit.
It might then have been cursed, yes, and even cut down and cast aside to be burned,
But never would it have been forced to bear not fruit,
But the Master Himself, as He endured His last hours in naked humiliation.
How dare humanity force the wood to be its accomplice in such dirty work!

As the soldier drew back his spear to pierce the side of Christ,
Did not the tree cry "Cut me instead! for I can bear His weight,
But not the burden of watching His pain, nor the sorrow of

---

[2] Copyright 1999. Thomas A. Robinson. All rights reserved.

Listening to His tired and labored breath as He hangs here so helplessly,
His sweating back supported by my splintery breast."

Was the tree relieved when Christ uttered, "it is finished;"
When His lifeless body was harvested from its supportive arms?
Or was it only left with sorrow; proximity to the creative Logos now lost?
As it was roughly disassembled, did it shudder as it was tossed in a heap
With the other instruments of death: the nails, the thorns, the whip?

Ah, but would not the God who loves and numbers the sparrows,
Who saved Abraham's son—though not His own—would not this God
Have eased the pain that day of all who suffered—even the lowly tree?
Within the stillness of that afternoon, did God not whisper to the tree,
And to the waiting world, words of a new Rosh Hashanah, a true atonement?

# 23

# The Power of Love

"T.E., Do you know who I am?"

My Dad spent his 91st birthday (8/11/2014) as he had spent most of the previous four years, and, as he would spend his remaining three months on this Earth, in a state of advanced dementia. As I have otherwise written, "Death is often the most patient of all our adversaries." Indeed, with our Dad, Death showed what seemed to be endless patience.

Several years before that birthday, he had lost his recollection of "his four boys." Some of my friends commented, "That must have hurt you deeply." I always answered, "No, not at all. The disease clouds those memories; It isn't his doing at all." We were also consoled by the fact that, for the most part, he didn't forget his "Dear Betty." "They'd had a long time to get used to each other," she would typically say. Indeed, by Dad's 91st birthday, Mom and Dad had been married for more than 71 years.

The dementia took Dad's memory; it did not take his essential gentleness. He never exhibited any of the aggression that is sometimes common among those who suffer from the condition. As he had been his entire life, he was sweet, kind, and gentle and, unlike his four sons, softly quiet.

> Love is patient; love is kind; love is not envious or boastful or arrogant or rude .... It bears all things, believes all things, hopes all things, endures all things (1 Cor 13:4, 7).

On the warm Monday that Dad turned 91, Mother, who lived in an apartment across the street from Dad's nursing facility in Northern Durham, maneuvered her walker across Carver Street and up the ramp to the building that housed our Dad. She entered his room and noticed that he was particularly calm and quiet. She talked to him for several minutes but noticed that he didn't reply. Sensing that this might be one of "those days" when the dementia caused him to be even more confused than usual, she took both his hands in hers, looked into his eyes, and said, "T.E., do you know who I am?"

Dad looked into her face for a full five seconds and then responded, "No .... But I DO know that I love you."

As St. Paul taught us, love endures all things. Hallelujah!

# 24

# Ebb Tide

"Can we go to the motion?"

When our son, Walker (who turned 40 several months before the publication of this book), was first putting his words together, he had an interesting take on what to call the large body of water off the coast of Hilton Head Island. Like most young children, he was fascinated with the ebb and flow of the water and so, either because he initially misunderstood what Jane and I had called it or, knowing Walker, because he thought he'd come up with a better word to describe the briny waters off the coast, he excitedly asked if we could "go to the motion?"

Indeed, there is something wonderfully hypnotic about the ingress and egress of our coastal waters; they seem to echo much of what we experience in our lives. Wall Street moves up and down. Our relative health comes and goes. Politically, each party experiences both victory and defeat. The tides move in; they move out.

Such ebb and flow is echoed in a Psalter selection that is often read during Lent:

When the Lord brought back the captivity of Zion,
We were like those who dream.
Then our mouth was filled with laughter,
And our tongue with singing.
Then they said among the nations,
"The Lord has done great things for them."
The Lord has done great things for us,
*And* we are glad.

Bring back our captivity, O Lord,
As the streams in the South.

Those who sow in tears
Shall reap in joy.
He who continually goes forth weeping,
Bearing seed for sowing,
Shall doubtless come again with rejoicing,
Bringing his sheaves *with him.* (Psalm 126).

Notice that the first three verses of the Psalm are written in the past tense. The Psalmist remembers when the House of Israel was restored to Jerusalem after the Babylonian exile. Their freedom had receded during the captivity; it rushed back with their return and their mouths "were filled with laughter," their tongues with "shouts of joy." The remainder of the Psalm gives the reader/hearer a clear indication that such laughter and joy are now in the past, for the Psalmist asks that their fortunes be restored. And he uses a particularly descriptive metaphor. There should be restoration "like the watercourses in the Negeb."

The Negeb — that southernmost portion of Palestine, the part that abuts the Sinai Desert — is dry throughout much of the year.

During the dry season, life is at an ebb. In the winter, however, the rains come, and the resulting flow of water spreads out and nourishes the entire area. We might remember that it was at the Negeb, probably during the fertile springtime, that the wandering Israelites first came into contact with the Promised Land. The paucity of their long wandering journey gave forth to abundance.

For the Psalmist, life is like the Negeb; it ebbs and flows, comes and goes. Earlier the people had been overcome in war. Many had been carried off to Babylon. But the Psalmist notes that they had been restored by the Lord. Their fortune had, overtime, waned again, but that was no sentence of death. God could — God would — restore things again.

Psalm 126 taught the people of Israel that times of sorrow would eventually give way to times of joy. It teaches us the same. There are happy days behind us. Sorrowful days may lie ahead. During Lent each year, as we look to Holy Week, we recognize that our Lord will endure much between Palm Sunday and Good Friday. There will be pain. There will be turmoil. There will be humiliation. But there will also be Easter! On Easter, we see what our Lord has done to Sin and Death, our mouths can be filled with laughter; our tongues can sing with shouts of joy.

## 25

# Cheers from the Sidelines

*"How can a guy in his 40s cry and long for the shoulder of his mother?"*

As they say, "The more things change, the more they stay the same." By that I mean, at least in part, that familiar patterns at play when I was a young boy are still in play with our grandchildren. Take Little League Baseball — by mid-summer each year, some of us within the multi-generation Robinson clan are pleading for someone to do just that, take Little League Baseball away, far away. Grandson Jack is actively involved in the sport right now. Fifty-five years ago, I was the catcher for Evening Optimist. Almost thirty years ago, Jack's Uncle Walker was a player in the Hillandale Northern-Durham league.

Hardwood bats have given way to those fashioned from aluminum. Metal cleats are no longer allowed. The safety equipment is much improved, but parents (and grandparents) still wildly cheer as youngsters compete at what used to be the national pastime. Life's lessons are still learned playing a noble game. Teamwork, cooperation, failure and success are all part of the process. If one looks carefully, one can occasionally get a glimpse of the Kingdom.

As I watched one of Jack's games last summer, my mind was drawn back to a hot, humid evening 30 years ago, when Walker's team was playing the second of two games at the Hillandale School field in Durham. We had arrived a bit early in order to scout the two teams that faced each other in the first game. That game was nearing its end. Because one team had a substantial lead over the other, both coaches were now substituting liberally. The coach for the batting team called for a portly, young lad to take his turn at the plate.

One could quickly discern that the young boy, who was wider than he was tall, wasn't ever going to make it to the major leagues. His practice swings were wild and erratic. His swings at the first two pitches thrown by the young pitcher confirmed that the lad probably had not made a hit all season. But the pitcher made a mistake with his third pitch. He threw it right where the stout little boy had wildly swung on the earlier pitches and the ball went off the boy's bat with a crack, shooting directly into the outfield, between two of the opposing players.

For almost anyone else the hit would surely have been a homer. I watched as the young lad ran down the first base line; I suppose you could call his labored gait "running." I watched as he turned at first base and headed toward second, his fists and arms pumping out of cadence with his legs. As he turned from second and headed toward third, now facing the small crowd in the third base bleachers, I thought, "I've never seen a youngster huffing and puffing like that in my life."

The boy's face was beet red and sweat beads had popped up on his forehead. His fat, little legs were pumping as fast as he could make them, although that wasn't very fast. For an instant, I thought the horrible. We are going to witness the world's youngest heart attack victim.

As I sat there, I saw a young woman leap down the steps of the bleachers and run to the fence bordering the field on the third base side. Built just like the youngster, undoubtedly his mother, I quickly thought that she — like me — must surely be worried about her son's health. Then I heard her yell at the top of her lungs, "Billy, run faster, run faster."

At that instant, you could see the expression change on the little boy's face. He missed his stride and almost stopped running between second and third bases. He didn't have to utter a word for many of us to know exactly what he was thinking. "MOM, I'M RUNNING AS FAST AS I CAN."

A lot of us, it seems, have a lot in common with young Billy? We spend our lives frantically running between second and third base, with well-meaning people on the sidelines yelling at the top of their voices, "Run faster, Billy, run faster."

A minister's spouse is diagnosed with a dangerous form of cancer. She is obviously apprehensive about the prognosis and the possibilities for her future. Fear fills her mind and her heart. She talks about her plight with a close friend who tells her if she'll just pray harder, God will cure her. She thinks to herself, "I'm already praying as hard as I can."

A young mother, rearing her children on her own because her husband has left her, finishes her working day and hurries out of the office or the classroom to get to her car so that she can pick up one of her children to take them to swimming practice. She laments to herself that it has been weeks since they actually sat down to an evening meal. Isn't that what family life used to be, sitting down at the supper table to go over the day's activities? She relates her frustrations to a friend who tells her that she just isn't sufficiently organized. If she'd just get organized, she would have the time to work at her job, take the kids to swim team, plan luscious suppers, and be beautiful all in the process — if she'd just get organized. She fights back the tears as she thinks to herself, "I'm already organizing as hard as I can."

A widow recalls the fact that she and her husband were married for more than fifty years. They had been inseparable — more than just husband and wife — they were best friends. Half a century had been spent doing things with each other *and for each other*. But now he's gone, and for her, life is just not as fun; it isn't a full; it isn't as fulfilling as it used to be. Most days she's just fine, but occasionally the loss overwhelms her. On those bad days, she feels bewildered and alone even when she is in the midst of a crowd of people. Many of us might tell her that she just needs to try a little harder on those days when life is gray. Try a little harder and you'll be able to cope, we might say. "But I'm already coping as best I can," she would lament.

When we come to church, sometimes we can be made to feel the same way. We can be made to feel that we are too worldly, too shallow, too selfish, too lazy, too apathetic, or too stingy. If this is the only message getting through to us from the Church, then the Church is no more than a mirror of what is beyond its walls.

Scripture and song tell us that "they'll know we are Christian by our love, by our love." Shouldn't that mean that we'll all be known by the shocking habits of our church, habits of encouraging one another, of building up one another, of affirming and celebrating one another? I say "shocking," because if any church would truly be such a place, then it would be shocking to the world around us; it would be a shocking example of what life in Christ can truly be.

The truth is that church should be a haven, a sanctuary, a place where we can all be encouraged in spite of our many failures. Most of us know when we fall short. We don't need anyone to tell us that we could have done better or try harder. We're already trying as hard as we can.

One of my friends who faces such a world confided in me that he was confused by all that was around him. The past few years have been hard. He felt tossed about like a cork in the ocean as a child became seriously ill, as his wife suffered a brief but serious illness, as he worked long hours to build an upstart business without any real assurance that those who worked around him were really committed to make it work. He confessed to me that he recently had done a strange thing. He'd gone into a darkened room, closed the door and prayed, prayed for some voice to tell him which way he should turn, what he should do, where he should go.

He said he cried. He cried uncontrollably. Turning to me, he said, "How can a guy in his 40s cry and long for the shoulder of his mother (she had died some years before)? We're supposed to be strong, assured. Christians are supposed to have it together."

Perhaps like me, you share the fears and frustrations of my friend. Like my friend, you may be running as fast as you can. What you may desperately need is to hear some gentle voice telling you that you needn't run faster, that you needn't try harder, that there's another Way. The marvelous thing is that there is such a gentle voice. It is calling to you today. It is so soothing and reassuring. It is so real, and it is so present.

There once was an itinerant preacher who said:

Come to me, all you that are weary and are carrying heavy burdens, and I will give you rest. Take my yoke upon you, and learn of me; for I am gentle and humble in heart; and you shall find rest for your souls. For my yoke is easy, and my load is light" (Matt. 11:28-30).

Christ calls us to his yoke. It fits us perfectly and individually. But we must respond in some way to receive it.

# 26

# Little Big Man: Zacchaeus' Child-Like Exuberance

"Then who can be saved?"

Each year, during Lent, as our *vision* follows Jesus and his movement toward the Cross, we begin to get a sense that our Lord's actions during Holy Week — actions that culminate in his death on Good Friday and his resurrection on Easter morn — are destined to turn the world upside down! Indeed, as St. Luke weaves his gospel toward the familiar story of Zacchaeus, we see that Jesus is not content with Jerusalem's status quo.

His biting parable of the Pharisee and the tax collector (Luke 18: 10-14) offers us what some New Testament scholars refer to as "subversive opposition," in which a "sinner" — the tax collector — is justified and the "righteous one" — the Pharisee — is regarded with absolute contempt.

Jesus continues by pointing out that his calendar isn't to be filled with appointments with the powerful and mighty; he has carved out his time instead for little children, "for it is to such as these that the kingdom of God belongs" (Luke 18: 16b). He adds that no one will enter the Kingdom unless they receive it as a little child.

That is the way of Jesus, to challenge the world to recognize that God's Kingdom belongs to those that society has forgotten or refuses to consider. The Kingdom belongs to those on the periphery. It belongs to the poor, to women — e.g., the widow of Nain (Luke 7:7-11); the woman who anointed Jesus (Luke 7:36-50); the woman with the 12-year hemorrhage (Luke 8:43-48); the women bent over for 18 years (Luke 13:10-17); the persistent widow (Luke 18:1-8); the woman who gave all that she had (Luke 21:1-4) — and to tax collectors. It belongs also to those who are lame or paralyzed, those who are lepers, or those, like the Samaritans, who live on the wrong side of the tracks. And the Kingdom belongs to children.

Indeed, the Kingdom particularly belongs to children — the ones who bring nothing but their innocence, who offer nothing but their powerlessness, who uniformly lack the sort of careful credentialing that the Pharisee has so carefully managed — because In God's Kingdom, as opposed to "our kingdom," the world's rules are subverted; the world itself is turned upside-down.

For any who desire to skip over Jesus' reference to the importance of receiving the Kingdom as a child, He continues: "How hard it is for those who have wealth to enter the kingdom of God! Indeed, it is easier for a camel to go through the eye of a needle than for someone who is rich to enter the kingdom of God" (Luke 18: 24b-25). We join those around Jesus in astonishment, wondering to ourselves, "Then who can be saved?" His reply: "What is impossible for mortals is possible for God" (Luke 18:27).

Finally, to show us that indeed, with God all things *are* possible — even an inversion of reality — Luke tells us the marvelous story of Zacchaeus (Luke 19: 1-9). It speaks to us on so many levels.

At one level, the visit to the house of Zacchaeus is a direct confrontation with the religious authorities who have already said that Jesus consorts with "tax collectors and sinners" (Luke 7:34). At another level, Jesus' act of approaching Zacchaeus represents communion with exactly the sort of "rich man" that Jesus has pictured in his earlier parable: the sort who has captured all the wealth around him and lost himself within that activity?

At a third level, we see the richness of irony represented by the interaction between Jesus and the "wee little man" named Zacchaeus. His name literally translates as "the clean one," yet Zacchaeus is anything but clean. He is tainted to his core. And like the tax collector in Jesus' parable, Zacchaeus *knows* that he is tainted; he knows that he's unclean. Zacchaeus longs for forgiveness.

Indeed, Zacchaeus longs for a God like that described in Psalm 130 — a God who doesn't mark every iniquity, but who offers forgiveness (Ps 130: 3-4). In Zacchaeus' world, a restored relationship with God is impossible for him and so, he longs for a God of the impossible, a God with the power somehow to pull Zacchaeus through the eye of the needle.

In Jesus, of course, that's exactly what Zacchaeus finds. Zacchaeus encounters the "Son of David." Moreover, Zacchaeus encounters the Son of Man, the Christ. Could the message of Jesus Christ really be true? Might even a sinner like Zacchaeus, the unclean one, be forgiven? Could "the clean one," in name only, be transformed from tainted to pure? Zacchaeus senses that in Jesus all things are possible and so how does Zacchaeus respond? He becomes "childish," acting like a kid. He actually climbs a tree.

Abandoning his pretensions as an important tax collector, a wealthy man, Zacchaeus, climbs a tree in his excitement to see Jesus. *He has become like one of the little ones!* And, true to his Word, Jesus reacts to Zacchaeus' childlike exuberance and says, "let's have a sleep-over" (my own loose translation of Luke 19:5). Zacchaeus has been pulled through the eye of the needle. Would that the rest of us could jettison our staid sensibilities!

# 27

# Prom Night

"Are you busy tonight?"

The young single mother looks down on the floor and picks up the thin little book of Bible stories. She thinks to herself that it sure has been a long time since she and the children have been to church. "In a few months, when things get back to normal, I think I'll start looking for a church home," she says to herself. "There is just too much going on in my life right now. Too many demands from others, too little help from friends, too much pressure on me," she decides. "But soon, very soon, we'll go back to church."

The retired businessman laments the fact that it has only been three months since his mid year's resolution and it is already broken. In June he had talked to the minister about his sense of loss. Without a routine of work each day, he just didn't seem to have the motivation to do anything. He told the minister he wanted to reach out to God, but he didn't know how. The preacher had suggested he begin a daily routine of journaling, of making specific, written notes about his prayer life, about his Bible reading, about his progress in learning to meet God at least half way. It had made such good sense and it seemed to work for a while. But you know how things go. Writing is difficult. Thinking is hard. Did he really have to read the scripture every day? Why not just on Sunday morning before Sunday School? That way it'd be fresh on his mind when he attended church. "Ah," the man thought. "I know what I'll do. I'll take a few months off from this journaling. I'm sure I'll do a better job after I've let my mind do some resting. When I am in a better frame of mind, I'll resume it and then I'll be able to continue it for a long time."

With regard to our two friends whom I've just described, should we say "Excuses, Excuses?" That sounds so harsh. After all, who can find fault with a young woman struggling against the forces of the 21st century or a retired gentleman who can't find the discipline necessary to approach God? Haven't we all gone through similar periods in our lives? As college students or as young married couples, didn't we use Sundays as a travel day? Or in more recent times, have we ever thought "Oh, why bother with all those church committee meetings! Someone else will be there to help make the decision, won't they?" Or perhaps, we have rationalized, "If I took that position as Sunday School teacher, or if I decided to see what the preacher looks like from the choir loft, gee, that'd take up part of my week in preparation, and I really am already stretched thin, aren't I?"

That's the way life is, isn't it? We have great intentions in our hearts and minds. We really mean to take the time, to expend the energy, to make the commitment to continue our spiritual journeying with God. But one thing or another seems to always get in the way. It isn't like we're some atheist who says there is no God. We're not some agnostic who doesn't care. We really do care, or at least we think we do. It's just that life is so complicated, and time is so short. If we can just be allowed to get our spiritual acts together, we'll do better, we promise.

You may have heard the oft-told story — how Satan was busy recruiting a new worker to sow seeds of discord on the Earth. He called three new recruits before his throne. He told them that he only had room for one more evil doer in the world, so he had to decide among them which would do the most damage to God's favorite creatures, man and woman.

The first said he should be chosen. Satan asked him what he would do. He said, "I'll tell the people there is no God, and then they will give up trying to serve Him." The Devil said, "Ah, many have tried that and it really never works, for in their hearts everyone knows that God is real."

The second prospect stepped forward and said, "I'll go and instead, I'll tell them there is no Devil." The Devil frowned and said, "Many others have tried that tactic and it never works either, for in their hearts, they know I exist."

The Devil looked over at his third prospect and inquired, "Well, what will you tell them?" This one said, "I'll just tell them that there is plenty of time." The Devil smiled and said, "Go forth, for you will wreak more havoc than all my other servants combined."

Then Jesus said to him, "Someone gave a great dinner and invited many. At the time for the dinner he sent his slave to say to those who had been invited, 'Come; for everything is ready now.' But they all alike began to make excuses. The first said to him, 'I have bought a piece of land, and I must go out and see it; please accept my apologies.' Another said, 'I have bought five yoke of oxen, and I am going to try them out; please accept my regrets.' Another said, 'I have just been married, and therefore I cannot come.' So the slave returned and reported this to his master. Then the owner of the house became angry and said to his slave, 'Go out at once into the streets and lanes of the town and bring in the poor, the crippled, the blind, and the lame.' And the slave said, 'Sir, what you ordered has been done, and there is still room.' Then the master said to the slave, 'Go out into the roads and lanes, and compel people to come in, so that my house may be filled. For I tell you, none of those who were invited will taste my dinner'" (Luke 14: 16-24).

Time - it's our great adversary. As if we didn't already have enough to be concerned about, time can cause us further problems. Time allows us to come up with Excuses, Excuses. It allows us to think we can give Jesus the answer of "Well, perhaps tomorrow." Excuses — time allows us to play games with ourselves. It can let us think we have come to this House for worship, when in fact, all we may have come for is fellowship. We can delude ourselves into thinking that our duty to God is fulfilled when we've had our ticket punched, when our coffee and donuts have been consumed, when we have patted each other on the back and sang a few hymns. There will always be TIME for a more complete commitment later, we think.

Excuses — time allows us to feel that we have completed our obligation to our neighbor when we, as a church body, have sent a few hundred dollars to feed and clothe the hungry. After all, there will be "time" later on for better, won't there be?

There will be plenty of time for our children or grandchildren to experience Christ. We need not do anything special now. Isn't it enough if we occasionally drop them by the church? That's what Bible School is for, isn't it? Time can convince us that it our responsibility to our children is completed when we have taken away the obstacles. We need not prod them toward God. They might resent us and anyway, there will always be time enough for that later, when they are more mature.

Excuses — time allows us to convince ourselves that Jesus will wait on us to get on with the program. But even though some of us act as if time will be around forever, instead it is fleeting, it is fast, it never lasts. In the parable noted above, Jesus is telling us all that time is not forever. Yet time is the measure of things on this Earth and eventually, sooner for some than for others, time runs out. For some of us, the deadline for putting aside our Excuses, Excuses may even be today.

Jesus is calling us, pleading with us, to set aside our Excuses and understand that the clock is about to strike midnight. Soon the carriages will turn back to pumpkins. Soon the satin and lace will only be spiderwebs. But Jesus is telling us also that while it's almost midnight, the celebration is not over. In fact, it is only now beginning.

Brenda had worked hard with the other members of the Junior Senior Prom Committee. For several weeks they had stayed late after school, gathering the necessary materials for props, decorating the high school student center. She had listened and smiled approvingly when the other girls described the dresses that they had purchased for that special evening. She overheard the boys talk about the tuxedos they had rented and the corsages they had picked out for their dates. She pretended she didn't hear about the special breakfast that had been planned at one of the girl's houses after the Prom, the most important night in one's high school years. She had watched each day pass as the magic night approached.

And now, it was Friday afternoon; the prom would begin that very evening at 8:00. She looked around the student center and gazed at the completed project and gave a heavy and pensive sigh. There was nothing left to do. Everyone would have a wonderful time that night, everyone except Brenda, of course. Brenda was nice and actually quite attractive, but Brenda stood six feet, one inch tall, and tall girls like Brenda just didn't get asked to the Prom.

She fought back a few tears as they made the last preparations. It was almost 4:30. The others were slipping away to fix their hair, to wash their cars, to complete those last-minute duties in anticipation of the evening.

Suddenly a figure slowly walked across the waxed and polished floor. It was Ernie, the shy, but very nice guy that everyone knew sort of, but with whom no one was really very close. Ernie tapped Brenda on the shoulder and quickly said, "Brenda, I was going to stay home this evening, because I don't really date very much, but I wondered: Are you busy tonight?"

Can you imagine the excitement in Brenda's voice as she squeals with enthusiasm, as she literally runs from the school grounds to her car to race home to tell her mother? Can you imagine the feeling within her as she and her mother quickly drive to the Bridal shop where her mother buys her a beautiful dress for the occasion? Can you imagine just how wonderful the Prom turned out for Brenda, how much she enjoyed the music, the dancing, those elaborate decorations, the conversation, that special moment?

Can't you see Jesus walking across the polished floor? He's slowly walking toward you and me. He's just tapped us on the shoulder. He's calling us to come with him, as his special guest. Have you ever had such a feeling in your life? He's inviting you and me and he doesn't care if we're tall and gangly, if we're old or young, if we're black or white, if we're lame or confined to a wheelchair.

He's calling us! He's calling us! Shouldn't we squeal with excitement? Shouldn't we go outside and shout the good news from the top of every hill we can find. The Prom's tonight and we've all been invited. In the name of the Father, the Son, and the Holy Spirit. AMEN.

# 28

# The Lion and the Hen

"Jerusalem, Jerusalem, ... How often have I desired to gather your children together as a hen gathers her brood under her wings ...?"

When C.S. Lewis needed a Christ-figure for his classic fantasy series, *The Chronicles of Narnia*, he chose Aslan, the lion. Those of you who are familiar with *Narnia* — the books or the movies — know that Lewis' choice was an excellent one for Aslan is at once, beautiful, noble, powerful, wise, brave, patient, and self-giving.

Learned scholar that he was, Lewis was no doubt drawing upon the fact that the lion was the symbol of the Hebrew tribe of Judah — the tribe that produced both King David and Jesus of Nazareth. In the final book in our Bible, we see another reference to this royal lion:

> Then one of the elders said to me, "Do now weep. See, the Lion of the tribe of Judah, the Root of David, has conquered, so that he can open the scroll and its seven seals (Rev 5:5).

Thomas A. Robinson

I'm taken by the fact that as Jesus approached Jerusalem in his final days, He offered up his own animal metaphor to describe himself, and it wasn't as a lion. Observe Jesus' language as seen in one of the traditional Gospel Lectionary options for the Second Week in Lent (Year C):

> At that very hour some Pharisees came and said to him, "Get away from here, for Herod wants to kill you." He said to them, "Go and tell that fox for me, 'Listen, I am casting out demons and performing cures today and tomorrow, and on the third day I finish my work. Yet today, tomorrow, and the next day I must be on my way, because it is impossible for a prophet to be killed outside of Jerusalem.' Jerusalem, Jerusalem, the city that kills the prophets and stones those who are sent to it! How often have I desired to gather your children together as a hen gathers her brood under her wings, and you were not willing! See, your house is left to you. And I tell you, you will not see me until the time comes when you say, 'Blessed is the one who comes in the name of the Lord'" (Luke 13:31-35).

I suppose that by the time Christ has entered Jerusalem for his final week, we would understand that His choices often aren't consistent with our own. For example, when Peter asks if forgiving someone seven times is sufficient — Peter's being more generous than us, is he not? Yet, Jesus offers up an alternative: seventy times seven.

When several of the disciples are sparring over which one will be on Jesus' right and which on his left in Heaven, Jesus posits that those who want to be first must be last. When the disciples wonder what an appropriate reaction might be if he or she was struck on the cheek by our enemy, Jesus gives them the improbable, "Turn the other cheek." When Jesus was asked about the appropriate response to someone who wants to borrow our shirt, His retort was that we should determine if the man or woman might also need our coat. When someone essentially asked Jesus what was the best way to save one's life, the Messiah responded, "Silly, try losing it."

And so it is, that when faced with the cunning of the fox named Herod, Jesus did not offer himself up as the king of the jungle. He showed no fangs, no claws, no powerful, thrusting muscles. He saw himself instead as a hen.

A hen's only weapon against the fox is her own body. The only protection she can offer her brood is to open her wings and hold her chicks unto herself. Steadfastly facing the fox, with one's wings wide open — it's a vulnerable position, is it not? Sort of reminds you of a man stretched out on a cross, doesn't it?

## 29

# Mary, Darlin', How Does Your Garden Grow?

"Master, did you not sow good seed in your field? Where, then, did these weeds come from?"

Some several years ago, a friend of mine decided that would be the year she'd launch her garden. Having grown up in a northern city, she had precious little experience with fresh vegetables except, of course, the kind that "grow" in the produce department at the grocery store. She'd driven through rural Iowa one summer and knew that corn there grew tall and green, but she'd never picked it, never experienced the itch of wet corn leaves and shucks as you move through a field in the summer.

She'd never had the "pleasure" of digging for potatoes or onions. Most of all, she'd missed the joys of weeding in the damp morning, before the sun gets too high to manage that menial chore. She's an academic sort, so late in the Fall, months before her actual venture into Nature, she perused the shelves at "the Regulator" on Ninth

Street in Durham and plopped down $40 for an award-winning book on backyard gardening.

Following the instructions to a "T," she roped off a small patch of her adequate back yard and carefully removed the Bermuda grass, being careful also to pull up the top four or five inches of soil, sift it for roots and weed stems, and replace it only after she'd mixed it with lime, compost, and manure. She rented a tiller and churned all this together and then let it rest through our mild winter.

Early the following spring, before it was actually time to plant most things outside, she got out some of her seeds and read the package instructions.

> Sow in trays in a warm place to maintain an optimum temperature of 72-84 degrees F. Gradually acclimatize to outdoor conditions for 10-14 days before planting.

Jesus' parable of the sower had not included such specific instructions. Hadn't the sower just broadcast the seed, allowing it to fall where it would? Oh, well, she thought. "Better follow the book" (err, I don't mean the "Good Book," but rather, the "$40 book").

Not wanting to leave anything to chance, she carefully planted – not sowed – her seed by hand. She carefully watered the garden each afternoon, waiting anxiously for signs of life. Then she left town for ten days during Duke's Spring break. Her helpful elderly neighbor, who'd been gardening for years, offered to watch out over her "spread" while she was gone.

When she returned ten days later, she found a thick patch of healthy young plants. Yet there was a problem: her "crops" didn't look like what she'd planted. The helpful neighbor identified a few of the plants as young tomato seedlings.

"Oh, those look great," he said. " You outta' stake 'em up in a couple of weeks."

"But I didn't plant any tomatoes. I don't even like tomatoes. Where'd they come from?"

"Most likely your compost, child," the neighbor explained. "It's what happens when somebody pitches tomato sandwiches onto the compost heap."

My friend and the neighbor recognized some of the other plants as morning glories, others as wild violets. The yellow squash was relatively easy to find, but there were several mysteries. What could she do? Rip it all up and start again? The long growing season in North Carolina would allow for such. Give up and let the Bermuda take it back as it surely would?

Master, did you not sow good seed in your field? Where, then did these weeds come from? (Matthew 13:27b).

My friend decided to follow the advice of the Parable: "let both grow together until the harvest" (Matthew 13:30).

Preparing the soil was only part of the story, it seemed. In fact, she'd prepared it so well that everything grew — the stuff she'd planted and the stuff that found its way there through the act of the unseen Gardener, blown by the wind or dormant in the soil until my friend's hard work made that plot of ground the perfect habitat for weed and honored morsel alike. A wild violet is a weed if you thought you'd have turnips; otherwise, it's a flower.

What if my friend's job in her garden, our job in ours, is not so much to select the seed, but to prepare the soil? Might it be that we are to give ourselves to the work without fretting so much about the results? One thing seems to be for sure: some Sower was there before

Thomas A. Robinson

my friend. There is more life within our world than most of us ever notice. We just have to stoop and look.

# 30

## Simeon's Story

"May I hold the baby?"

My close friend — and theological sparring partner — Jim Sutherland, retired recently after almost four decades of OB/GYN medical practice. I suspect that Jim long ago lost count of the number of babies that he delivered. The number has to be significant since, in additional to having an active, vibrant, private medical practice for many years, Jim also spent five years or so in a frenetic, indigent medicine hospital setting in Atlanta. During that period of time, Jim's work week often consisted of 90 to 100 hours, delivering babies for mothers who had no resources, who typically had no husband — mothers who had often enjoyed little, if any, medical care during their pregnancies. Many nights, Jim slept — to the extent that he could steal a few quiet hours — in what amounted to a small, hostel area near the public hospital's maternity ward.

Suffice it to say that Jim has held a lot of babies. He's greeted robust, healthy newborns that have had the advantage of excellent prenatal care. He's also carefully cradled others, some weighing just over a pound, who arrived far too early into this all-too-scary world.

Despite Jim's confidence — I think one has to be confident to be a great obstetrician like Jim — he confesses that he never lost his sense of awe at seeing a "new" human being take his or her first breath, utter the first sound, and either accept or protest the change of circumstances from Mother's sheltering womb to the demanding landscape of life.

On many "birthing" occasions, particularly during those years in which Jim was delivering the offspring of indigent mothers, he'd quietly sing "Amazing Grace," as he tended to both mother and newborn. Jim can't carry a tune in a bucket, but that didn't matter. Considering the circumstances, he just thought it was the appropriate thing to do.

He and I have often talked about the powerful and particular perspective that he had as an obstetrician. Jim allows that none of us asks to come into this world and very few of us ever later ask to leave it. He has added that no matter what the circumstances of birth, in a true sense a newborn is a blank slate. He or she is perfect potential. What will be remains to be seen. Will the child live a long, healthy, productive life? Will it instead see mostly sadness and/or tragedy? Will it be surrounded by a loving, nurturing family or will it suffer from neglect or abuse?

I once asked Jim if he'd like to be able to look into the face of the newborn and see what lay ahead for the child? Jim quickly retorted, "No; just as I am happy not to know my own future, I'm the same with newborns. It's just better not to know."

In Luke's Gospel, we see the story of a man — an old man, actually — who looked into the face of an infant and did see what lay ahead. As much as we might like to link the Christ movement — the Christian faith — only to the positive, the uplifting, the beautiful and peaceful, we must also face the inescapable: when the light of Christ is illumined, it also casts shadows. Indeed, as one of America's greatest preachers has allowed regarding the presentation of Christ at the Temple to Simeon, Luke has woven a "dark thread into what has been a bright tapestry of hopes, inspired songs, and prophesy" (Fred B. Craddock, *Luke: Interpretation*, A Bible Commentary for Teaching and Preaching, John Knox Press, 1990, p. 39).

As many of us remember, Simeon, "righteous and devout" (Luke 2:25b), had prayed for years for the consolation of Israel. Scripture teaches that the Holy Spirit descended upon him and revealed to him that he would not see death until he had seen the Lord's Messiah.

Shortly after the birth of Jesus, guided by the Holy Spirit, Simeon visited the Temple in Jerusalem. When Mary and Joseph brought the infant into the Temple, as was the Jewish custom, one supposes that he said to Mary, "May I hold the baby?" Luke indicates that Simeon took the infant up into his arms and said:

> Master, now you are dismissing your servant in peace, according to your word; for my eyes have seen your salvation, which you have prepared in the presence of all peoples, a light for revelation to the Gentiles and for glory to your people Israel (Luke 2:29-32).

Just getting used the fact that they were parents, Mary and Joseph were amazed at what the old man had said about their son. If this was true, then the angel who had visited each of them before the birth of Jesus must be right. Indeed, this child — their child must be the Anointed One. What marvelous news!

Alas, as Mary had indicated in her Magnificat (Luke 1:46-55), the coming of the Messiah is not "good news" for everyone. The powerful will be brought down from their thrones. The proud are scattered; he has filled the hungry with good things and sent the rich away hungry. Simeon looks into the eyes of the child and sees the future, sees even the Cross, and says to Mary:

> This child is destined for the falling and the rising of many in Israel, and to be a sign that will be opposed so that the inner thoughts of many will be revealed — and a sword will pierce your own soul too" (Luke 2:33-35).

The story ends there. I suppose that Simeon handed the baby back to his mother with not a little portion of uneasiness. As he departed the Temple, I wonder if he did so with less peace in his heart than he had anticipated.

# 31

# The Prophet Peggy

"What if there was a place where you could go and there was no TV, and you could break bread, and whoever you were sitting with was family?"

As some of you know, I was a *Mad Men* devotee. I didn't watch the show during its first season in 2007, but hearing all the flutter at that season's close, I bought Season 1 on iTunes and I immediately swallowed the hook. I think it was mostly my age. Like some of you, as I watched each episode, I could remember the events that formed the backdrop of the show: the anti-tobacco legislation, the Kodak "Carousel" slide projector, the Kennedy assassination, the Vietnam war, and the early Nixon years.

As *Mad Men* entered its seventh and final season (aired in 2014), the year depicted was 1969 — my senior year in high school. A year had passed since the fateful '68 Spring when MLK, Jr. was shot and killed, since the summer of RFK's assassination, since the August riots in Chicago during the Democratic National Convention, and since Nixon's thumping of Humphrey in November.

Thomas A. Robinson

It's 1969 and the mad men and women have been chasing the bus for years. By that I mean when the dog chases the bus, what does it do if it catches it? After all, the bus isn't edible. The partners at Sterling Cooper Draper Pryce (Don, Pete, Peggy, Joan, Roger, *et al.*) have been chasing the bus for years and now, for better or worse, they've caught it. But what do you do when you've caught it?

If you recall the story lines of *Mad Men*, you know that the final Season 7, most of the characters have fallen into the trap described by Paul Tillich, the German-American existentialist-theologian of the same time period (he died in '65). Tillich wrote (*see, e.g. Dynamics of Faith*) that all human beings have a natural urge to seek out the Ultimate, that in the process of that search, they often focus on various "ultimates" (notice the lower case "u").

Many of us are quite familiar with these ultimates: the career, the Mercedes, the villa at the beach or in the mountains, the comfortable pension or the board room, the corner office, tenure, or the prominent pulpit. It isn't that there is anything inherently wrong with such pursuits; it's that they're "ultimates", not *the* Ultimate.

Tillich described the low point that is inevitable for anyone seeking out after the ultimates. He called it "existential depression," the feeling — no, the heartfelt knowledge — that, like Esau, you've sold your birthright for something much less than Ultimate. And so, what you experience isn't just depression — it's depression at the existential level since the pursuit has cost you everything and the reward has left you empty.

That's where many of the characters in *Mad Men* found themselves in the final season of the show. They were in the throes of a deep, poignant, existential sort of depression — a depression so deep they couldn't name it. They had chased after the ultimates and they had caught them. And yet, their prize wasn't at all Ultimate.

## Questions of Faith

In the penultimate scene of episode 6 (entitled "The Strategy," aired 5/18/2014), two of the main characters, Don and Peggy, sit in Don's office sipping scotch. The offices around them are empty; it's Sunday, after all, and everyone is supposed to be enjoying the success that the firm's business has wrought.

Don and Peggy are discussing the pitch the firm will make the following week as they seek to attract Burger Chef as a new client. The firm is losing Chevrolet and they really need this new client, or at least, they're sure that they need the client. Expressing her latest effort at crafting a 30-second spot, Peggy allows that their marketing research has pointed out an incongruence: that 60's moms are supposed to cook supper every night for the family, that both the man of the house and society at large look down on a woman who needs the night off, even if she's worked all day in an advertising office.

How, ponders Peggy, do you pitch the idea that it's ok for the family to go out to Burger Chef and grab a burger and fries? Peggy yearns for 1955, when television — and the ads that pay Don's and Peggy's lucrative salaries — wasn't a constant distraction, when women didn't have bumps on their heads from collisions with glass ceilings, when fathers knew their roles, when times were not so complicated (as I watched the episode, I recall thinking just how much more complicated things had become in the years since '69, and I'm sure I said, "oy vey").

Peggy takes another shot of scotch, looks at Don and says, "What if there was a place where you could go and there was no TV, and you could break bread, and whoever you were sitting with was family?"

"Bingo," Don says; that's the pitch they'll use for Burger Chef.

Wow ..., if there was really such a place? Consider what Paul wrote to the struggling souls in the Corinthian church:

> For I received from the Lord what I also passed on to you: The Lord Jesus, on the night he was betrayed, took bread, and when he had given thanks, he broke it and said, "This is my body, which is for you; do this in remembrance of me." In the same way, after supper he took the cup, saying, "This cup is the new covenant in my blood; do this, whenever you drink it, in remembrance of me." For whenever you eat this bread and drink this cup, you proclaim the Lord's death until he comes (1 For 11:23-26).

There is, of course, such a place. It's too bad that both the "place" and the world around her often fail to recognize that present fact. The "place" is Christ's Church and by "church," I don't mean a particular parish or congregation, I mean Christ's holy, catholic Church, the Church within which weekly we say that we believe. Perhaps along with me, you share a deep sense of sadness in the acknowledgment that the world doesn't instantly recognize the Church as a place to which one can safely retreat, a place that does *not* echo the distractions of our culture, but rather is divorced from them, a place where one can break bread — very special bread — and where, because baptismal waters are so much thicker than blood, everyone around you is family.

A minister friend of mine once told me that he was convinced that much of a Christian's life is spent in lament. Maybe so. I certainly lament that Don Draper, who knows the pulse of the world around him better than any of the other *Mad Men*, didn't immediately say to Peggy, "We can't compare a hamburger stand to such a place; people already know that place is the Church." I can lament the fact that he didn't say it; I understand completely that he didn't.

All too often the Church has been satisfied with the little sliver that the world has allowed us. "Give us a few hours on Sunday," we often say, "and we'll give you, the world, the rest of the week." We've expected too many church leaders to become effective chief executive officers, instead of presbyters or prophets. All too often we have ordered our spiritual world and our spiritual lives by utilizing the same organizational concepts that have proven "successful" in the "real world," all the while forgetting that the so-called "real world" is devoted to ultimates, but never to *the Ultimate*. We've deluded ourselves into thinking that there are Twelve Keys to an Effective Church (*see* Ken Callahan's book by that title), all the while knowing that no matter how many the keys, there's only one Way (one Truth, One Life).

Take a quick inventory of the people with whom you come into contact each week. How many Peggys do you know? How many friends or colleagues yearn for a place that is divorced from the so-called cares of the world, a place where one can break bread, a place where all those around you, no matter what their last name, or the strength of their wallet, or their gender, their sexuality, or the color of their skin are embraced as family?

There are so many Peggys around us. You and I know them. Let us pray that trusting God and living in Christ, we can love them all by showing them what true Communion with God and with each other is really like. It could be an experience with the Ultimate.

# 32

# Waiting for the Lord

*"What Now?"*

I have told some of you about my wonderful cousin Jan. She was born in 1950, about a year before Todd and me, and because she was our first cousin, we saw a lot of her in our growing up years. Jan was stricken with cerebral palsy shortly after her birth. Because of the severity of the disease in Jan and because of her early age at the time she contracted it, she never developed very much. Never more than 40 pounds or so, she was never able to talk, never able to walk, never able to control her arms or legs, never able even to hold her head erect on her own. And yet, she lived almost 26 years — 26 years in which my Uncle Harold and Aunt Betty fed her baby food — 26 years during which they changed her diapers.

Because of her special needs, some of the physicians advised Harold and Betty early on to put Jan in some sort of long-term care facility, some institution — my Aunt and Uncle understood that to mean some place "out of the way" — so that they could get on with their lives, could get on with the responsibilities of raising Jan's younger brother Rob, who was born a few years later.

But you see, the ones making the recommendation didn't have the benefit of the special vision of my Aunt and Uncle; that is, the ability to see beyond the surface of things, to the reality that lay within.

To them Jan was a special daughter, a child with tremendous and long-term needs, yes, but a daughter who could respond to their love with a smile, someone whose face brightened when she saw her brother, Robbie. That's the reality that Uncle Harold and Aunt Betty saw. And so, Jan was always a special part of our growing up, a special part of our Thanksgiving or Christmas celebrations, a special cousin for my three brothers and me. And since Jan went to church every Sunday that I can ever remember, she was a special part of the little Presbyterian church within which I grew.

Aunt Betty and Uncle Harold held up well over those many years. The circumstances didn't make them bitter or sad. They did the best they could, and Harold and Betty's best was wonderful.

There were those days when it was particularly tough, however. There was the day all the other children Jan's age went to first grade. There was the day the children Jan's age said the catechism at Olney Church. There was her sixteenth birthday, the day Aunt Betty realized that under different circumstances, Jan would have excitedly gone to get her driver's license. And there was prom night, a special evening when all the others Jan's age were either putting on fancy prom dresses or rented tuxedos.

On those special, difficult days sometimes Aunt Betty, and at other times Uncle Harold, would ask themselves the natural question, "Why can't Jan be like the others? Why can't she run and play? Why can't she drive a car? Why can't she go to the prom?" As I say, those special days were tough for them, but to their credit, they didn't lash out at anyone because of their pain.

In spite of the passage of now more than forty years, I remember Jan's funeral as if it was yesterday. The rural church was wonderfully filled to celebrate the passing of one of God's children. We sang several songs and shared the words of our wonderful Lord who said, "Let the children come to me; do not try to stop them; for the kingdom of God belongs to such as these" (Luke 18:16).

We drove from the church in a pouring summer rain. As we turned through the gates of the cemetery, Buck Dixon, long-time friend of the family, fellow Olney church member and police officer, stood by his squad car, rain and tears pouring down his face, his hat not covering his head, but held instead over his heart in strong and deep respect for the passing of tender Jan.

At the graveside, we heard again the restorative words of the prophet Isaiah:

> Have you not known? Have you not heard? The Lord is the everlasting God, the Creator of the ends of the earth. He does not faint or grow weary; his understanding is unsearchable. He gives power to the faint and strengthens the powerless. Even youths will faint and be weary, and the young will fall exhausted; but those who wait for the Lord shall renew their strength, they shall mount up with wings like eagles, they shall run and not be weary, they shall walk and not faint (Isaiah 40:28-31).

After the burial, as is the custom in the South, the family went over to Betty and Harold's. We made ourselves busy with the sorts of things people do after funerals. We gathered some food, shared some idle chatter, and reminisced a bit. And Aunt Betty put her arm around my Uncle's waist and he in turn put his around her shoulder. She looked at him and with a tender smile she asked, "What now?"

And he turned to her and said, "Now? ... Now she's like the others."

The ability to see beyond the limitations offered by the world; it's a gift to those with Faith. And so, dear friends, in the time of the resurrection (*see* Luke 20: 27-38) to whom does Jan belong? Well take heart friends, for like you and me, like my Grandmother Lib, like "T.E." and countless others who have gone on before us, she is like the angels. Thanks be to God for the promise of the resurrection.

# About the Author

Thomas A. Robinson received his B.A., *cum laude*, in both Economics and History in 1973, from Wake Forest University, his J.D. in 1976, from Wake Forest University School of Law, where he served as Managing Editor, *Wake Forest Law Review*, and his M.Div. in 1989, from Duke University Divinity School. From 1976 to 1986, Tom was in private law practice, focusing on workers' compensation defense work. In 1986, he and his family moved to Durham, N.C., in order that he could matriculate at Duke Divinity School. Intending to stay in Durham for three years and then return to Western North Carolina, Tom and Jane have lived in the Bull City now for 32 years (and counting).

For the past 30 years, Tom has managed a delicate balancing act — mixing an active professional "secular" life with the sacred. A nationally-recognized legal scholar and writer in the field of occupational injuries and illnesses, Robinson is co-author of *Larson's Workers' Compensation Law*, the preeminent legal treatise on the subject. For many years, he also handled copyright and publication matters for Duke University School of Law, Duke University Press, and the American Institute of CPAs.

## Thomas A. Robinson

Since Tom's "Div School days," he has carved out significant time for the sacred, first as a part-time local pastor at Asbury UMC (Durham, NC, 1987-1993), then as pastor/teacher for the Riverside Gathering (a post-denominational congregation without walls, centered in Durham, NC, 1993 to the present), and as an *"ex officio"* preaching/teaching resource at Trinity Avenue Presbyterian Church (Durham, NC, 2002 to the present).

Known by friends as a master of the poignant tale, Robinson has rarely met a story that he didn't love. His favorite story is told within the gospel of John.

www.ingramcontent.com/pod-product-compliance
Lightning Source LLC
Chambersburg PA
CBHW030323080526
44584CB00012B/682